The American Manifesto

A Unifying Vision

Steven C. Flanders

To Tony

Much Thanks

Steve C. Flanders

Sword of the Spirit Publishing

615 473-4037

ISBN: 978-0-9838836-5-4

Published by Sword of the Spirit Publishing
www.swordofspirit.net

Dedicated:

To Melvin Kasselman, Dick Goggin, Ray Flanders, and the whole long parade of unsung American patriots.

Contents

Preface and Acknowledgements

The American Manifesto: A Unifying Vision

I guess you could say that I started writing this book on the day President John F. Kennedy was murdered: November 22, 1963.

I was ten years old, living in Colorado Springs, the oldest son of a Catholic Democrat and predominantly Irish family. I remember my father staying up all night and rejoicing the night Kennedy won the Democratic nomination. I also remember my sister leading me and my younger brother in prayer at lunchtime the day he was shot.

The conclusion I came to that day was that something was terribly wrong with this country. Without knowing what, I knew the American system of government was not operating the way it should. I've been looking for what went wrong since then.

I'm happy to report that I've identified the malfunction(s) and how to fix the problem. That's what this book is about.

Probably the best way to begin is to examine my personal journey through the universe of political philosophy and how I came to these conclusions. This will also enable me to acknowledge a couple of folks who enlightened my way and greatly advanced this work.

After 1963, I eventually became involved with the anti-war movement. Along about 1965, as opposition to the Vietnam War got mainstream media attention, this gung ho 12-year-old was angry at the protesters. One day I read an article about a protest in which the protester urged people who wanted to understand his objections to the war to read the Constitution. This sounded like a fair challenge, so I did read the Constitution and found that indeed, the Vietnam War was being conducted without following constitutional guidelines. I was against the war from that point on.

Over the next few years, I attended a number of anti war rallies. I was always surprised and saddened that I was unique, the only one at the rally that was there defending the Constitution. Folks would say that it was an immoral war, but never had an answer when I noted that if a proper declaration of war had been required previous to any military action in Vietnam, there never would have been a moment when the people of

America could have been persuaded to go to war in Southeast Asia.

My political activism expanded to include civil rights issues and environmental concerns. By the mid 1980's, I was something of a veteran of left wing politics, living in the San Francisco Bay area. Still involved with progressive causes (precinct committee person for Dukakis in 1988), I detected a deep flaw in liberal thinking. All of the activist groups were always calling for an increase in community and community spirit. However, I noticed that every policy measure they supported called for more big government programs, which, I began to realize, destroy community spirit.

No longer convinced of liberalism, and yet not conservative, I was kind of a philosophical orphan when I moved to Denver in 1989. There I soon met the first person I want to acknowledge, Mr. Dick Goggin. Dick, who passed away some years ago, was an old cold warrior, John Bircher type, who greatly increased my appreciation of the Constitution. He gave me in-depth tutelage on the subject with a special focus on the Tenth Amendment.

He not only convinced me that the Constitution had been abused on a wholesale basis, but I began to wonder if the return to local control and responsibility that would follow along with a return to a proper use of the Tenth Amendment wouldn't be a way to revive that precious community spirit. So I started being a conservative and a Constitutionalist at that. But I was a conservative with a couple of big twists. First of all, as my friends chided me, I had been driven to my conservatism by my passionate liberal inclinations.

The second twist started on one of the early days of my conservatism while sitting over at Dick's house, perusing his copy of the Constitution. Seeing it for the first time through the lens that every word meant something specific, and that it should be adhered to as much as possible, I came upon the First Amendment.

When I read the old familiar words to the liberal's favorite amendment with new eyes, a chill came over me. I remembered that when I was in school I would ask what those words meant because it was unclear, and the teachers would always answer (I asked the question more than once) that it meant freedom of speech and press and separation of church and state.

Now with my new eyes, I saw that if the words of the First Amendment were observed strictly, then the congress, and by extension the entire edifice of the federal government, should not have any role in what I suddenly saw as the powers of moral self government. I began to suspect that restoring the powers of moral self government to the states and localities by returning to an honest use of the First Amendment, would, as in the case of Tenth Amendment issues, work to strengthen community spirit. So I forged into the 1990's as a conservative activist with some unique ideas about the First Amendment.

Then the second person I want to acknowledge, someone I have never met, came along. Around 2001, I read *Unequal Protection*, a book by Thom Hartmann about the rise of corporate personhood in 1886, and it launched my thinking into new realms. I had heard vague references to this issue, but his thoughtful analysis opened my eyes again. I instantly saw that the doctrine of corporate personhood was the missing piece that completed the puzzle, and that would cause this concept of community self government to appeal to both liberals and conservatives. The more I considered the whole concept, the deeper and broader it grew, and the more sensible it became. But now I was no longer a conservative or a liberal but once again a political orphan. That's when I decided to write *The American Manifesto*.

Be forewarned though, that while this is a unifying vision that can provide a foundation for our nation to grow together into the future, it is strong and bitter medicine. In the Biblical book of Revelation, chapter 10, verse 9, the author John is told to eat a book that "shall make thy belly bitter, but it shall be in thy mouth as sweet as honey". This book is the opposite, in that it will probably taste bad going down, at least in spots (it is almost impossible to conceive of any modern American, left or right, who won't be deeply offended by some part or another of this book), but once it is all taken in, it will become very sweet, satisfying, and hopefully, inspiring.

Finally, I want to acknowledge some more folks. First of all, I want to thank my family and friends for putting up with my wild eyed theories all these years. My friend Sandy Titus deserves special thanks for providing me a platform on which to hone my writing skills by publishing "The Denver Dialogue". Mike Feliton, Marc Chavez, and Chelsea Glaeser earned my thanks by wading through a dreadful first draft and giving some invaluable feedback.

Mike Berry is a friend and brother who gave me a sounding board for years. My publisher, Donald James Parker, is a new found friend and brother, sent it seems, by divine appointment. Finally, I want to thank my heavenly Father, and his only begotten Son, my Lord and Savior Jesus Christ, without whom none of this would be possible.

Steven Flanders
February 22, 2012
Nashville, Tennessee

Introduction

"Where there is no vision, the people perish..."
Proverbs 29:18

A vision, in the political sense, sustains and preserves the people in two fundamental ways. First, a true vision of governance will unite the many different people of good will, the folks who want a fair and stable government. Second, a viable vision of government will show the way that those united people might proceed to attain the promise of the vision. This manifesto is an attempt to provide both aspects of a vision to the American people.

The United States of America in the early part of the Twenty-First Century faces many dire challenges; some would even say we face threats to our very existence. For the most part, our political system seems to be failing us, unable to solve the problems with both sides of the political spectrum merely recycling the same non solutions with every passing year and decade. This failure is due not so much to avarice or stupidity on the part of our leaders, but to the fact that in the course of the last 150 years or so, we have slowly painted ourselves into a corner. We have allowed our political process to be taken hostage by special interests and a wealthy merchant class We have, in the process, come to accept a failed concept of governance. Over the course of these changes, we have lost sight of the guiding principles, the vision of government that this nation was founded on. Restoring that vision of liberty is the multi faceted purpose of this *American Manifesto*. The hope is that we, the people, can once again see the following aspects of our society

1. That we might see how this nation was designed to function, and how that functioning was far superior to what we have today.

2. That we might see how that superior way of doing things has been lost to the minds of the American people. It has been lost by a process that has grown around three wrongheaded misuses of the federal judiciary over the course of the last one hundred and fifty years.

3. That we might see how reasonable it would be to reverse those errors. We merely have to go back and take the correct path on the trail of history, re-founding our government on those same principles of local community moral self government we started with. This could be accomplished, for the most part, simply by returning to adherence to the United States Constitution as written.

4. That we might see that there is a feasible, peaceful and orderly strategy whereby we might actually get this high-minded, revolutionary agenda established in law.

It is as though our grandfather left us an old model T out under a tarp in the back yard. We have but to put in the work, clean up, lubricate and tune that old vehicle to get it running again. The metaphor goes on too, because while that old model T, even if restored, might not be the best possible vehicle imaginable, it is still the best of all the current governments in the world today. When we look around the world and see the wicked state of decay in the governments of the world, we see that the vehicles of those other systems can be likened to Stone Age donkey carts compared to the machine age model T we could have. Then that model T starts to look pretty good. What's more, once we got that old thing up and running, we could modify it and give it all the latest hi tech improvements we could envision.

It has been said that the biggest problem confronting modern civilization is that our morals and ethics haven't kept pace with our technological development. Just a glance at the world's problems, from industrial development causing climate change to problems around the proliferation of nuclear weapons to health issues such as abortion, stem cell use, cloning and genetic engineering, reveals to anyone who is paying attention that there is a problem. We humans still haven't come to grips with the right and wrong, the ethics and morality, of how to use all this new technology. What is worse, the pace of technological growth, and the subsequent moral challenges that raises, continues to accelerate, while the growth in our moral and ethical thinking seems to be slowing down, or even regressing.

So whether the industrial revolution is a blessing or a curse on the human race remains an open question. It is not a question of if the technology can be developed but rather a question of whether it should. That then becomes an issue of governance, specifically whether or not the people of this planet can regain control of government, and thereby control of technology. Interestingly, and for reasons that will be expounded, this is not a question that can be solved by the failed political vision that brought about the current political matrix of left versus right, or by deciding which policies to institute at the federal level.

Instead, the solution lies in regaining the original vision of American self government. With that vision regained, and that form of government re-founded, we have the promise of a much more involved and enlightened citizenry. That would engender deliberations in the halls of government that are much more holistic, wide ranging, and flexible, and less bound by narrow legalisms and the influence of special interests. With that kind of a handle on government, we would be able to get a handle on the powers of runaway commercial greed, bringing that powerful force into a much more healthy form of community accountability. With that handle on commerce, we might finally be in a position to get a rein on the industrial revolution, and be able to insist that the advances of technology be a blessing to all of humanity, and not the bane and curse they have become to so many.

Again, restoring that vision of the American system of liberty and government, and showing the way to re-establish that system is the subject of this manifesto. In regaining that original vision of the American system of liberty and self government, we will have to face up to and debunk some precepts that have wrongly come to be seen as foundational to our system. In actuality these (now seen as sacred) principles are parts of a process that has brought about the dismantling of American liberty. The substitution of a false vision of governance has caused us to lose sight of our starting vision and of the blessings of liberty that accrue to any people when a system of free self government is properly executed.

One quick aside is in order because some will undoubtedly attack this as just another conspiracy theory. While it must be admitted that the dismantling of the American experiment in government might have been the work of a conspiracy, it is pointless, divisive, and therefore not constructive to use the analysis of conspiracy. Rather, let's think of ourselves as a people who have been making our way through a trackless wilderness these many years. In a few instances, we took the wrong paths, and they have led us into dead ends and the corner we are currently painted into. Why we took the wrong path, whether due to stupidity, ignorance, prejudice, or because some evil people conspired to mislead us, is beside the point. The point is to go back, if we can, and get on the right path now.

It has been a long slog down this path with, seemingly, barely a whisper that we might be going the wrong direction. Along the way, many of us have become emotionally attached to some sacred cows (wrong headed precepts) that will shortly be gored. The only consolation offered is that the soon to be gored sacred cows belong to both the right and the left of our revered two party political divide. Among these wrong-headed precepts, these wrong turns we have taken in the path, are three major blunders which I'll focus on first. There are a number of smaller, peripheral issues that follow along with the major blunders, which will be looked at later.

One: The idea that free enterprise (capitalism) as conceived by the founders allows unbridled greed and runaway power to be accumulated by big interstate and international corporations. This was never the founder's intention or part of the system they founded, as will be seen.

Two: The idea that the central, federal government is the best repository for the social functions of government, "the great almoner of public charity throughout the United States". This includes issues from education and health care to public relief and economic security for the elderly. All of these flow from the basically socialistic idea that the federal government should be the provider of last resort. We will explore how devastating this misplacement of some of the powers of government has been, how unconstitutionally they were established and how they have worked to erode the natural bonds of community and family.

Among the other programs to be debunked in this area, Social Security, that most sacred of all sacred cows, will be prominently gored.

Three: The third major blunder to be exposed will be the mistaken notion that The United States of America is founded on the concept of a separation of church and state. The legal, constitutional, and philosophical fallacies involved with the federal government usurping the powers of moral self government and of the courts seizing the power of deciding the issues of religion, morality, speech, and press will be looked at closely. Later, it will become evident how pursuing this impossible myth of separation of church and state has empowered a particular belief system at the federal level of government which is directly counter to the purpose for which the founders wrote and ratified the First Amendment. We will also examine the way that this federal usurpation of the powers of moral self government weakens the bonds of community, degrades the citizenry, and leads us away from liberty and into the clutches of authoritarian government.

These three principles, which have come to be seen as inviolable foundational principles, have in fact worked, individually and with a negative collective synergy, to dismantle the original plan of government that American liberty was founded on. Once we have come to the vantage point of seeing that negative synergy in action, we will then be able to see larger patterns in the evolution and changes in all human government. We will behold downward spirals of government and see how one false principle lays the groundwork of social decline, which leads to another bad policy later. We will also see that, thankfully, there can also be positive synergies and upward spirals where just the opposite happens, and that we might take advantage of those positive spirals to solve our many problems.

One of the ways this phenomenon of a synergy in government was noted by some of the American founders, leaders like John Adams, George Washington and others, is the idea that only a moral people will be able to keep a free government.

"We have no government armed with power capable of contending with human passions unbridled by morality and religion. Avarice, ambition, revenge, or gallantry, would break the strongest cords of our Constitution as a whale goes through a net. Our Constitution was made only for a moral and religious people. It is wholly inadequate to the government of any other."

President John Adams, October 11, 1798. [1]

This is an obviously true principle of government, because only a people who have a strong moral self restraint, who will freely choose to do the right thing, will allow themselves to remain free. If that sense of moral self restraint diminishes beyond a critical point, where the masses begin to cast off restraint, a downward spiral of government will be set in motion, and those same masses will soon accept, probably welcome, and maybe even demand, authoritarian government.

The great point of this manifesto is that the reverse of that principle is also true, in a profound way. I.e.; just as only a moral people can remain free, only a truly free and self governing people will see the reasons to be moral. There needs to be a another quick aside here, because this use of the term "morality" isn't intended to entail any particular religious or philosophical belief system, but rather is defined, here, to mean that the citizens are upright and well intended toward government and each other, sincerely trying to make the system work, rather than trying to see what they can get out of it and get away with. This echoes what John Kennedy said at his inauguration, "Ask not what your country can do for you, but what you can do for your country." This sense of "morality", or as phrased in other places, this municipal spirit, or these republican virtues, are absolutely essential if any free system of popular self government is to be sustained, and not fall prey to the siren song of authoritarianism.

From that point flows the certain claim of this "American Manifesto" that the only architecture of government likely to produce those involved, upright, moral citizens, which will set in motion a positive spiral of governance, is the architecture of local community moral self government. Happily, that form of government is the same form of government defined by the United States Constitution and contained in the original American vision of liberty. So, as usual, we Americans are greatly blessed. To restore to ourselves those lost blessings of liberty, we don't have to tear our system down and build another, but rather we must simply use our system the way it was intended to be used.

The call here is for us to try this American experiment one more time, get the old thing cleaned up, lubricated and running, and thereby not only regain the blessings of liberty, but have a good chance to get the twin beasts of runaway corporations and an out-of-control industrial revolution back on short leashes of community accountability.

One more note. To show that we have learned from our historical mistakes, and to make sure everything works out best for everyone, as we set about to re-establish a nation based on liberty and justice for all, it is imperative that we be sincerely inclusive about the "all" part this time.

Footnotes

[1] *America's God and Country Encyclopedia of Quotations*. Ed. William J. Federer, (FAME Publishing Inc.Coppell, TX, 1994), p.10

Chapter 1

Corporate Personhood Emerges Into Law

"The defendant corporations are persons within the intent of the clause of section 1 of the Fourteenth Amendment to the Constitution of the United States, which forbids a State to deny to any person within its jurisdiction the equal protection of the laws."

Quoted from the court reporter's head notes
Santa Clara County v Southern Pacific Railroad
(118 US 394). May 10, 1886

The first of the three major changes, usurpations actually, that have brought about the near collapse of the American republic was the establishment, in 1886, of the concept of corporate personhood. As the heading of this chapter states, because of that status as persons, corporations suddenly received the protections under the Fourteenth Amendment, reserved to all natural persons. Thus, they essentially came out from under the regulation of the states and localities, (Because the states weren't allowed to put any controls on corporations that they didn't put on individual humans) and were able to operate across state lines, form monopolies, lobby legislatures, and gain much more power than they had previously been allowed. Corporate personhood, and the social and political changes that followed in its wake, even though it seems a minor footnote in history, must be examined more closely. This is because it constitutes the opening salvo in what has been a dismantling of the system of self government originally handed down from the founders of this nation.

First we will look at how corporate personhood came about, and then we will examine how it has acted like a kind of engine of destruction, driving the dismantling of the American experiment. We will also take a quick glance at how corporations were controlled before 1886, and why that was a far healthier system for all concerned.

The facts of the matter are fairly straightforward, even though they have been obscured by the mists of time, and a few questionable court precedents. The book entitled *Unequal Protection: The Rise of Corporate Dominance and the Theft of Human Rights*, can not be recommended highly enough at this point The author, Thom Hartmann, literally wrote the book to describe how corporate personhood came into being. As such, please indulge a few paragraphs of what amounts to a book report on the subject.

According to Hartmann, the founders were well aware of the dangers of monopoly business, as the Boston Tea Party had been as much a protest of monopolistic business practices as it was a response to the British government's taxation policies that allowed that monopoly.

"Reading Hewe's account, I learned that the Boston Tea Party resembled in many ways the growing modern day protests against transnational corporations and small town efforts to protect themselves from chain store retailers or factory farms. With few exceptions, the Tea Party's participants thought of themselves as protesters against the actions of the multinational East India Company and the government that "unfairly" represented, supported, and saved the company while not representing or serving the residents."[1]

Furthermore, some of the founders went so far as to propose that a prohibition on monopoly be included in the Bill of Rights, even though that idea was rejected in favor of allowing regulation of corporations to remain at the state and local level.

The following passage was included in a letter from Thomas Jefferson to James Madison in 1788:

"I sincerely rejoice at the acceptance of our new constitution by nine States. It is a good canvas, on which some strokes only want retouching. What these are, I think are sufficiently manifested by the general voice from north to south, which calls for a bill of rights. It seems pretty generally understood, that this should go to juries, habeas corpus, standing armies, printing, religion, and monopolies." [2]

Earlier, other founders had made similar statements. In 1777, Samuel Webster asserted, "Let monopolies and all kinds of oppression be guarded against. [3]

During the Constitutional convention, there were concerns, as Mr. Gerry, of Massachusetts objected to the proposed Constitution, in part because "Under the power over commerce, monopolies may be established." [4]

Shortly thereafter, during the national debate about ratifying the Constitution, the Massachusetts ratifying convention proposed some additional amendments, including "Fifthly, that Congress erect no Company of Merchants with exclusive advantage of commerce." [5]

"But the Federalists fought hard to keep 'freedom from monopolies' out of the Constitution. And they won." [6]

The way it stood, at least until around 1886, was that states, not the federal government, could regulate corporations, because they could control the chartering process however they wanted.

"...in Wisconsin—as in most other states at that time: (1800's)

*Corporations' licenses to do business were revocable by the state legislature if they exceeded or did not fulfill their chartered purpose(s).

*The state legislature could revoke a corporations' charter if it misbehaved.

*The act of incorporation did not relieve corporate management or stockholders/owners of responsibility or liability for corporate acts.

*As a matter of course, corporation officers, directors, or agents couldn't break the law and avoid punishment by claiming they were 'just doing their job' when committing crimes, but instead could be held criminally liable for violating the law.

*State (not federal) courts heard cases where corporations or their agents were accused of breaking the law or harming the public.

*Directors of the corporation were required to come from among stockholders.

*Corporations had to have their headquarters and meetings in the state where their principal place of business was located.

*Corporation charters were granted for a specific period of time, like twenty or thirty years (instead of being granted 'in perpetuity', as is now the practice).

*Corporations were prohibited from owning stock in other corporations in order to prevent them from extending their power inappropriately.

*Corporations real estate holding were limited to what was necessary to carry out their specific purpose(s).

*Corporations were prohibited from making any political contributions, direct or indirect.

*Corporations were prohibited from making charitable or civic donations outside of their specific purposes.

*State legislatures could set the rates that some monopoly corporations could charge for their products or services.

*All corporation records and documents were open to the legislature or the state attorney general.

Similar laws existed in most other states." [7]

Think of how far these, and similar laws could go toward reining in runaway corporate greed. (Some states also had laws against any individual sitting on the board of more than one corporation). Nonetheless, much of this state and local regulation of corporations was negated by the establishment of corporate personhood, which was done in a very sly and underhanded way in the case of *Santa Clara County v Southern Pacific Railroad* (118 US 394). In that case, the court ruling said absolutely nothing regarding corporate personhood, but in the heading of the case, where the clerk of the court added explanatory notes, he inserted a couple of statements (one of them appears at the head of this chapter) regarding corporate personhood, which were later adopted into American case law by being wrongly cited as precedent.

As Hartmann writes, "No laws were passed by Congress granting that corporations should be treated the same under the Constitution as living, breathing human beings, and none have been passed since then. It was not a concept drawn from older English law. No court decisions, state or federal, held that corporations were persons instead of artificial persons. The Supreme Court did not rule, in this case or any case, on the issue of corporate personhood." [8]

Notwithstanding, the precedent was wrongly cited, and by the time the mistake was discovered, it was considered too late to correct it. Because corporations were considered persons, all the protections and immunities guaranteed to persons under the Fourteenth amendment had to be extended to corporations, even though most folks at the time the Fourteenth was ratified thought it was intended to protect freed slaves. Gaining personhood rendered corporations immune to most state and local regulations.

Hartmann puts forth three plausible theories about how this blunder came about. His favorite theory claims the clerk did it. Mr. John Chandler Bancroft Davis was the Clerk of the Court, a position of notable stature at that time. Mr. Davis was an author and lawyer, and a great friend of the railroads, being at one time on the board of directors of a railroad. As such, it is hard to believe that he would insert the concept of corporate personhood into a Supreme Court ruling without understanding the consequences.

A second theory is that one of the Justices on the Court, Mr. Justice Stephen J. Field, helped to arrange things, since he was at the same time still sitting on the bench of the Ninth Circuit Court of Appeals of California where the case originated. Justice Field was a highly ambitious man, another great friend of the railroads, and known to advocate for corporate personhood.

The third theory involves the former U.S. Senator Roscoe Conkling and former U.S. Representative John A. Bingham, both of whom were actively involved in drafting the Fourteenth Amendment. Both of these men later testified that they had intentionally used the word "person" instead of the phrase "natural person" in the text of the Fourteenth precisely so that it might later be used to establish the personhood of corporations.

It appears that all three theories hold water, and that indicates that big business, especially the railroads, were engaged in skullduggery and mischief. That then points to a deeper theory about how all this came about, which is that the invention of a radically new technology, i.e. the locomotive, gained the owners of that new technology so much wealth that they were able to change the balance of political power in their favor.

At the time of the advent of railroads, many saw the great promise of cheaper transportation of people and freight, but also saw the threat of too much corporate power. Consequently, some states, especially those in the South, established limits, as noted in the book, *Gangs of America*, by Ted Nace.

"Well into the 1850's, southern railroads were largely adjuncts to canals, rivers, and sailing ships. Legislators wrote charters that prevented railroad officers from forwarding goods to other railroads or steamships. Many charters allowed city councils to define where railroads had right of way and thus allowed town merchants to choose the location of railroad junctions and company wharves. These charter restrictions ensured that gaps between railroads were large enough for merchants to take advantage of breaks in transit." As quoted from historian Scott Reynolds Nelson. [9]

While this was admittedly less efficient, and may have been merely the result of the jealousy of other commercial interests, it did work to keep railroad owners from getting too much influence over the political processes of those states. That has to be contrasted with states like Pennsylvania where the arguments for large scale efficiency won out, and in a few short years the Penn Central Railroad began to dominate the Pennsylvania state house.

Concurrent with that concentration of wealth and power, the Civil War broke out. Northern industrialists in general, and railroads in particular did very well in the war. Congress went so far as to fund the construction of a transcontinental railroad in that era. All of this added even more to the immense wealth of the railroads, and corporations as a whole.

Because of that nearly limitless wealth, the railroads could take shot after shot after shot at the courts and state and national legislatures to gain even more advantages. Santa Clara County was not the first case heard before the Supreme Court where railroad lawyers tried to get the court to declare that corporations were persons; it's just the first case where the plan worked. They had the motivation, since corporate personhood would take them off the leash of community accountability. They had the means, since they had almost unlimited wealth with which to bribe, cajole, lobby and otherwise influence public officials. They had the opportunity since they could bring any number of cases to trial. Eventually they were able to commit the crime.

Of course, personhood wasn't enough. Around the same time, the idea that a corporation could be doing business in any number of states but only be controlled by the regulations of the state they were headquartered in came into vogue. That created a charter mongering race to the bottom, where states started to out do each other in making accommodations to corporate greed. This is the big reason why, even today, so many corporations are headquartered in Delaware.

Many have noted what happened at that time, and even saw some of it coming. Once again in *Gangs of America*, Ted Nace writes:

"Sociologists call the 1897-1903 period "the corporate revolution." But as we have seen, the real corporate revolution took place over a longer period, roughly from 1850-1900. During this revolution, larger corporations did not merely come to dominate the American economy. More significantly, the legal structure defining the corporation as an institution was fundamentally altered. A century earlier, the framers of the American system of government had attempted to devise a "containment vessel" for corporate power: the state-issued charter. Now that system was completely disassembled and replaced with another whose goals were the exact opposite—as though the steel bars that had formed a cage were melted down, recycled, and used to create a suit of protective armor instead. Rather than protect democracy from corporate power, the legal system increasingly shielded corporations from legislative power." [10]

Abraham Lincoln in a letter of Nov. 21, 1864 to Col. William F. Elkins saw it coming.

"We may congratulate ourselves that this cruel war is nearing its end. It has cost a vast amount of treasure and blood. The best blood of the flower of American youth has been freely offered upon our country's altar that the nation might live. It has indeed been a trying hour for the Republic, but I see in the near future a crisis approaching that unnerves me and causes me to tremble for the safety of my country.

As a result of the war, corporations have been enthroned and an era of corruption in high places will follow, and the money power of the country will endeavor to prolong its reign by working upon the prejudices of the people until all wealth is aggregated in a few hands and the Republic is destroyed. I feel at this moment more anxiety than ever before, even in the midst of war. God grant that my suspicions may prove groundless." [11]

Lincoln had been a great friend of the railroads and big business up to that time, but one can assume that he saw the corporate beast, which had previously been such a beneficial servant of the people, was slipping off the leash of community control, and threatened to become the people's master. He wasn't the last leader to warn of the threat of runaway corporate power.

"On December 3, 1888, President Grover Cleveland delivered his annual address to Congress. Apparently, the President had taken notice of the SANTA CLARA COUNTY decision, its politics, and its consequences, for he said in his speech to the nation, delivered before a joint session of Congress, 'As we view the achievements of aggregated capital, we discover the existence of trusts, combinations and monopolies, while the citizen is struggling far in the rear or is trampled to death beneath an iron heel. Corporations, which should be the carefully restrained creatures of the law and the servants of the people, are fast becoming the people's masters." [12]

In 1939, more than fifty years later, and more than seventy years after the ratification of the Fourteenth Amendment, Justice Hugo Black made the following observation.

"Of the cases in this court in which the Fourteenth Amendment was applied during its first fifty years after its adoption, less than one half of one percent invoked it in protection of the Negro race, and more than fifty percent asked that its benefits be extended to corporations." [13]

To sum up this section, the Clerk of the Supreme Court, Mr. John Chandler Bancroft Davis composed the words that have been wrongly cited as precedent for corporate personhood, ignoring the fact that he had no power to make such proclamations.

To once again borrow from *Unequal Protection* by Thom Hartmann

"And there it was in the notes. The very first sentence of Davis's note reads, 'The defendant corporations are persons within the intent of the clause of section 1 of the Fourteenth Amendment to the Constitution of the United States, which forbids a State to deny to any person within its jurisdiction the equal protection of the laws.'

That sentence was followed by three paragraphs of small print that summarized the California tax issues of the case. In fact, the notes by Davis further down, say, 'The main—and almost only—question discussed by counsel in the elaborate arguments related to the constitutionality of the taxes. This court, in its opinion *passed by these questions* (emphasis added), and decided the case on the question whether under the constitution and laws of California, the fences on the line of the railroads should have been valued and assessed, if at all, by the local officers, or by the State Board of Equalization...' In other words, the first sentence of 'The defendant Corporations are persons...' has *nothing* to do with the case and wasn't the issue that the Supreme Court ruled on.

Two paragraphs later, perhaps in an attempt to explain why he had started his notes with that emphatic statement, Davis remarks, 'One of the points made and discussed at length in the brief of counsel for defendants in error was that 'Corporations are persons within the meaning of the Fourteenth Amendment to the Constitution of the United States.' Before argument Mr.

Chief Justice Waite said: 'The court does not wish to hear argument on the question whether the provision on the Fourteenth Amendment to the Constitution, which forbids a State to deny to any person within its jurisdiction the equal protection of the laws, applies to these corporations. We are of the opinion it does.'

A half page later, the notes ends, and the actual decision delivered by Justice Harlan begins—which, as noted earlier, explicitly says that the Supreme Court is *not*, in this case, ruling on the constitutional question of personhood under the Fourteenth Amendment or any other amendment." [14]

In that way, the communities of America had the power of economic self determination taken from them. Even though the blunder has been found out, we are told it can't be undone, that it is set in stone forever.

This brings up a short but radical aside. It seems that any skullduggery or mischief that gets accomplished can never be undone, but protections on the people's liberty and security, no matter how wise their crafting or legitimate their establishment, seem to always be up for change and negotiation. Perhaps we should re-think that mode of doing the people's business.

Pre-Corporate Personhood

To maximize the impact of that re-thinking, it will be appropriate to look at the way corporations used to be regulated in this country since it has been asserted that the way Americans dealt with corporations before the advent of corporate personhood in 1886 involved a healthier and more constructive system. Let's develop that theme a little here.

Consider the original concept of incorporation. LLC stands for Limited Liability Corporation, and it means that the folks who have invested their money in some particular enterprise can be held liable, if the enterprise fails, only for what they have invested, and not for their entire personal fortunes. This is a good idea, as it encourages the development of new technologies and industries since the investors aren't forced to risk their entire life's savings. Because of that protective privilege, many investors are willing to put their money into new, risky ventures, ventures which may well yield new jobs and wealth for many people.

Since a corporate charter is granted as a privilege by government, law makers consequently have a duty to ensure that this artificially created beast (which can't die or feel pain) doesn't do harm to the people.

Before 1886, protection was ensured through the free reign endowed to local and state governments to grant and pull charters as they deemed appropriate.

As has been seen, the states put many controls on corporations that are considered unconstitutional today. What's even more important, since the state legislatures and local governments could, under public pressure, be induced to pull the charters of any corporation that was seen as getting out of its chartered role or of misbehaving and being detrimental to the community, the corporations engaged in a lot of self policing to ensure that the public saw them as benefiting the community.

Essentially, the reason this pre-corporate personhood way of doing things was better (and we will look at it in more depth in later chapters) was that we didn't come to the process of controlling corporations in an adversarial mode of consumer versus worker versus manager versus owner versus government officials. Instead, we sat down at the same table as equal citizens and worked together to decide how this new technology/ enterprise could benefit the community. As equals at that table, the participants could examine every possible aspect and impact of the proposed corporation such as livability of wages, workers' health, environmental impact, and distribution of profits. Once those decisions had been made, the corporate officials would do a lot more self policing to adhere to those guidelines because their protection lay, not in the legalistic mode of courts, legislation, and high paid lawyers, but in the community with the good will and even admiration of the people. After all, without that image and reality of being a good corporate citizen, any state or locality could pull the corporate charter and kill that particular profit making beast. In that mode, things weren't seen so much as a capitalism versus the workers struggle, but instead successful businessmen were seen as heroes and pillars of the community.

That is how it worked, and it worked well. That is why even a man as wise as Abraham Lincoln became such an enthusiastic supporter of corporations and railroads before they got too powerful. Free enterprise, industry and commerce generated prosperity for all, and yet the dangers of excess wealth and power were avoided by community control of corporations. It was a system that was good for all and liked by almost all. However, there was an alarm sounded by Alexis DeTocqueville in the 1830's.

"For all this conventional enthusiasm and obsequious formality toward the dominant power, it is easy to see that the rich have a great distaste for their country's democratic institutions. The people are a power whom they fear and scorn. If some day the bad government of democracy were to lead to political crisis or if ever monarchy appeared as a practical possibility in the United States, one would see the truth of what I'm saying." [15]

The political crisis they were looking for was the American Civil War and the growth in corporate power that followed. With the advent of corporate personhood, the "rich" took their chance to dismantle the "democratic institutions" that they had such a great "distaste" for. Then, not only did the corporate beast get off the short leash of community control, but the resulting exponential growth in the power of big business set in motion a process that resulted in a dangerous concentration of political power in the hands of the federal government.

Regardless of whether corporate personhood was born of conspiracy or happenstance, it has since its inception worked to increase the power of big business. Not surprisingly, the establishment of corporate personhood in 1886 was followed closely by the Robber Baron, monopolies and trusts era of the 1890's and early 1900's, when the forces of corporate greed gained ascendancy over the people's government and society in general.

Decline of State and Local Government

By allowing monopolies, combinations (what are today called conglomerates) hostile takeovers by one corporation of another, and any number of other practices that were regulated and or prohibited by the states before corporations gained personhood, corporate personhood has worked like a destructive engine to diminish the importance of local and state government in the hearts and minds of the people.

To better understand how this happened, let's consider a couple of writings that came from the hand of author and social critic Jack London. In 1908, Jack London's book, *The Iron Heel* was published wherein the firebrand socialist author presented the strongest of cases for a socialist takeover of capitalism.

While we look at a few passages from that novel, keep in mind that the speeches and discussions he used in it were taken from real life debates and speeches he made, as his daughter, Joan London, wrote in his biography.

"Few of Jack London's books, even those which were consciously autobiographical, are so intensely personal as *The Iron Heel*. Ernest Everhard was the revolutionist Jack would have liked to be if he had not, unfortunately, also desired to be several other kinds of men. His best knowledge of the class struggle and the socialist movement, his best speeches and essays he gave to Everhard, as well as the achievements of other men." [16]

As such, the following passages should be considered a frank and honest discussion of conditions as they existed in the early 1900's.

In the chapter, "The Machine Breakers", a title he generated from his accusation that small businessmen of the early 1900's were essentially Luddites, bent on rolling back the clock to an earlier day that favored them, the character "Ernest" represents the views of Mr. London.

"Especially interesting was Mr. Asmunsen's narrative of his tribulations as a quarry owner. He confessed that he never made any profits out of his quarry, and this, in spite of the enormous volume of business that had been caused by the destruction of San Francisco by the big earthquake. For six years the rebuilding of San Francisco had been going on, and his business had quadrupled and octupled, and yet he was no better off.

'The railroad knows my business just a little bit better than I do," he said. "It knows my operating expenses to a cent, and it knows the terms of my contracts. How it knows these things I can only guess. I must have spies in my employ, and it must have access to the parties to all my contracts. For look you, when I place a big contract, the terms of which favor me a goodly profit, the freight rate from my quarry to market is promptly raised. No explanation is made. The railroad gets my profit. Under such circumstances I have never succeeded in getting the railroad to reconsider its raise. On the other hand, when there have been accidents, increased expenses of operating, or contracts with less profitable terms, I have always succeeded in getting the railroad to lower its rate. What is the result? Large or small, the railroad always gets my profits."

"What remains to you over and above," Ernest interrupted to ask, "would roughly be the equivalent of your salary as a manager did the railroad own the quarry."

"The very thing," Mr. Asmunsen replied. "Only a short time ago I had my books gone through for the past ten years. I discovered that for those ten years my gain was just equivalent to a manager's salary. The railroad might just as well have owned my quarry and hired me to run it."

"But with this difference," Ernest laughed; "the railroad would have had to assume all the risk which you so obligingly assumed for it."

"Very true," Mr. Asmunsen answered sadly. [17]

A little later in the same chapter, after a discussion of profit and competition, "Ernest' is speaking again.

"You make small-capitalist speeches such as Mr. Calvin made. What did he say? Here are a few of his phrases I caught: 'Our original principles are all right,' 'what this country requires is a return to fundamental American methods-free opportunity for all,' 'The spirit of liberty in which this nation was born,' 'Let us return to the principles of our forefathers.'

"When he says 'free opportunity for all,' he means free opportunity to squeeze profits, which freedom of opportunity is now denied him by the great trusts." [18]

The fictional "Mr. Calvin" probably did mean that, in 1908, and that is the great tragedy. With the advent of corporate personhood, resulting in a lack of corporate accountability to community, free enterprise itself became both a runaway destroyer of community, and seen as the enemy of the people. No one at the time seemed to realize that the change had been wrought in 1886 in the Santa Clara case, but instead, virtually everyone bought into the conventional wisdom of the day that big capital had suddenly gotten greedy. Even the most left wing and progressive writings of the early 1890's might bemoan the rise of monopolies, but took no cognizance of the 1886 case.

To continue with the passage from *The Iron Heel*:

"No one answered for a long time. Then Mr. Kowalt spoke.

'What are we to do, then?' he demanded. 'To destroy the trusts is the only way we can see to escape their domination.'

Ernest was all fire and aliveness on the instant.

'I'll show you another way!' he cried. 'Let us not destroy those wonderful machines that produce efficiently and cheaply. Let us control them. Let us profit by their efficiency and cheapness. Let us run them for ourselves. Let us oust the present owners of the wonderful machines, and let us own the wonderful machines ourselves. That, gentlemen, is socialism, a greater combination than the trusts, a greater economic and social combination than any that has as yet appeared on the planet. It is in line with evolution. We meet combination with greater combination. It is the winning side. Come on over with us socialists and play on the winning side.'

Here arose dissent. There was a shaking of heads, and mutterings arose.

'All right, then, you prefer to be anachronisms,' Ernest laughed. 'You prefer to play atavistic roles. You are doomed to perish as all atavisms perish. Have you ever asked what will happen to you when greater combinations than even the present trusts arise? Have you ever considered where you will stand when the great trusts themselves combine into the combination of combinations- into the social, economic, and political trust?'

He turned abruptly and irrelevantly upon Mr. Calvin.

'Tell me,' Ernest said, 'if this is not true. You are compelled to form a new political party because the old parties are in the hands of the trusts. The chief obstacle to your Grange propaganda is the trusts. Behind every obstacle you encounter, every blow that smites you, every defeat that you receive, is the hand of the trusts. Is this not so? Tell me?'

Mr. Calvin sat in uncomfortable silence.

'Go ahead,' Ernest encouraged.

'It is true,' Mr. Calvin confessed. 'We captured the state legislature of Oregon and put through splendid protective legislation, and it was vetoed by the governor, who was a creature of the trusts. We elected a governor of Colorado, and the legislature refused to permit him to take office. Twice we have passed a national income tax, and each time the Supreme Court smashed it as unconstitutional. The courts are in the hands of the trusts. We, the people, do not pay our judges sufficiently. But there will come a time—'

'When the combination of the trusts will control all legislation, then the combination of the trusts will itself be the government,' Ernest interrupted." [19]

Once again, neither Mr. Calvin, Ernest, nor the author, Jack London, seemed to realize how much the basis of a healthy, community oriented free enterprise, one of the original pillars of American liberty, had been dismantled with the imposition of corporate personhood.

Consider this second passage, a political essay from Jack London's pen

"Antagonism never lulled revolution, and antagonism is about all the capitalist class offers. It is true, it offers some few antiquated notions which were very efficacious in the past, but which are no longer efficacious. Fourth-of-July liberty in terms of the Declaration of Independence and of the French Encyclopedists is scarcely opposite today. It does not appeal to the workingman who has had his head broken by a policeman's club, his union treasury bankrupted by a court decision, or his job taken away from him by a labor-saving invention. Nor does the Constitution of the United States appear so glorious and constitutional to the workingman who has experienced a bull pen, or been unconstitutionally deported from Colorado. Nor are this particular workingman's feelings soothed by reading in the newspapers that both the bull pen and the deportation were preeminently just, legal, and constitutional. 'To hell, then, with the Constitution!' says he, and another revolutionist has been made—by the capitalist class." [20]

Clearly, from the point of view of Jack London a mere twenty years after the imposition of corporate personhood, he saw the American republic as having failed in its mission to protect the working people from abuse at the hands of big capital, and to ensure that the industrial revolution was a blessing, and not a curse, on the lives of the people. More to our point, since he didn't seem to even be aware how greatly the principle of corporate personhood had changed the landscape of American politics, he held local and state governments to be irrelevant, seeking change at the national, or even international level.

This phenomenon of people becoming alienated from a part of government that has lost real power is natural and inevitable, as is shown in this passage from *Democracy in America* by Alexis DeTocqueville.

"It is important to appreciate that, in general, men's affections are drawn only in directions where power exists. Patriotism does not long prevail in a conquered country. The New Englander is attached to his township not so much because he was born there as because he sees the township as a free, strong corporation of which he is part and which is worth the trouble of trying to direct.

"It often happens in Europe that governments themselves regret the absence of municipal spirit, for everyone agrees that municipal spirit is an important element in order and tranquility, but they do not know how to produce it. In making municipalities strong and independent, they fear sharing their social power and exposing the state to risks of anarchy. However, if you take power and independence from a municipality, you may have docile subjects but you will not have citizens." [21]

The thinking in the early 1900's probably was that since the counsels of the local community are rendered impotent by a federal mandate that corporations can only be regulated in the same ways as natural persons; why bother with local government? The individual is left vulnerable to the excesses of corporate greed and can resist corporate oppression only by involvement with the national political process.

Increasingly, because local and state powers were usurped to federal control, the people saw local and state governments as somehow obsolete. Progressive thinking was that since corporations could operate with impunity across state lines, the only way to control them was with some kind of federal powers. This thinking paved the way for Teddy Roosevelt and the Progressive era.

The first great tragedy in this narrative is that no one in the progressive movement seemed to consider returning the powers of economic self determination to the states and locals. This would have been a much safer and more effective way to curb corporate greed. Instead, led by the great "Trust Buster", Theodore Roosevelt, we moved in the far more dangerous direction of putting our trust in, and granting massive political power to a distant central government.

The first and most famous of these new federal powers was the Sherman Anti-Trust Act that has only been sporadically effective in slowing the growth of corporate power, and rolling back a few individual monopolies. On the other hand, due to the ongoing problems of corporate personhood, charter mongering from state to state, and in modern times international trade agreements like NAFTA and the WTO, the overall power of corporations as a whole has continued to grow unabated.

Peripherals

At the same time, since the people were losing confidence in local government to protect their interests, a host of peripheral changes occurred, concentrating many more powers in the federal government.

Spurred on by a campaign in the Hearst newspapers concerning corruption in the medical profession, the federal congress passed the Food and Drug Act of 1905. These changes usurped from the states the powers to license and regulate the medical profession, and mandated a prescription system for controlling the distribution of drugs. This has paved the way decades later for a crisis in health care and brought about calls for even more federal involvement in the lives of individual citizens.

Since we had lost the consciousness of having fifty separate state minds heard in the senate, (a concept borrowed from the Iroquois) the direct election of senators, which makes the senate less, and not more responsive to the will of the people, gained enough popular support to be ratified as the 17th Amendment. This amendment virtually ensures that the organized and self aware voice of the masses is never heard, but rather both houses of congress became venues for the individual to be just a face in a popular mass, only able to address the federal congress as one among three hundred million. With the direct election of senators, each senator is no longer held under the check of having to answer to an organized and empowered body of thinkers back in the home state, (the various state legislatures) who don't want to surrender any more of their prerogatives than they absolutely have to.

When the constitution was first written, the Senate was conceived as the more thoughtful, deliberative body, so it was considered wise that they have terms of six years, and be appointed by the state legislatures. This appointment process was to keep them somewhat above the tumult and short term thinking of partisan politics. Because of their role as the more deliberative of the two bodies of the national legislature, they were given the powers to confirm many presidential appointments, and to ratify treaties. While the Senators were tied to their home states, and they could easily be recalled by the home legislatures that appointed them, it was probably good to have them ratifying treaties. However, since they now sit with virtually no one to answer to, except the masses, once every six years in mass media dominated elections, that treaty ratifying power is extremely dangerous. Under Article 6 of the Constitution, any treaty that is ratified becomes the law of the land, the constitutions or laws of the state notwithstanding. With the advent of the United Nations, and its bent for concocting social policy by treaty, this treaty ratifying power in the hands of a very unaccountable senate becomes the source of a great deal of mischief. Far reaching social policies can be enacted without the consent of the governed.

Another far reaching peripheral change made in this era was granting the federal government the power to collect a revenue tax directly from individuals. While this tax placed directly on individuals ran contrary to the constitutional prohibition on such a tax found in Article 1, section 9, sentence 4 of the Constitution, it was rendered legitimate because it was itself established by constitutional amendment, the Sixteenth Amendment.

Nonetheless, even though it was done constitutionally (notwithstanding that some question the legitimacy of that ratification) it was still a profoundly anti-American concept. To understand how the founders viewed the federal government, and how they sought to control it, it will be instructive to think of the federal government in this instance as a huge, powerful bear wearing big wooly mittens. Such a beast is very well equipped for fighting off a foreign enemy, especially if we remove the mittens. Even with mittens in place, that huge and powerful bear is very good at controlling and punishing the small beasts, likened to dogs and cats, which correspond to the states and localities. But when it comes to dealing with individuals, the mitten clad bear is very bad at catching and controlling the individual ants that represent the individual citizens. This is how the founders intended it, so that the distant, powerful, and least accountable level of government would have virtually no direct dealings with the individual.

With the establishment of the Internal Revenue Service, we in effect took the mittens off the bear, and handed it a pair of tweezers. Now, it can not only deal with us ants as individuals, but it has the power to look at the most intimate details of our personal financial lives. Thus, we individual Americans are not only put at the mercy of a distant, unaccountable government, but that same government now has an unending stream of revenue that is uncontrolled by any other authority. This allows federal officials to engage in any scheme they want to, and answer to no one. This is unwise and anti-American in the extreme.

The final major peripheral change brought about in the first couple decades of the Twentieth Century, in an era when the public was losing confidence in local and state government, was the establishment of the Federal Reserve System. This central bank, so opposed by leaders like Thomas Jefferson and Andrew Jackson was voted on in the middle of the night on a Christmas Eve. Befitting such an auspicious birth, it unconstitutionally abrogated Congress's power to coin money and regulate the value thereof (Article 1, section 8, (5)) giving it to a quasi-governmental group of private bankers. Handing control of the money supply over to some corporate bankers is once again a very unwise and anti-American move that would have horrified the founders of this nation.

The legality of these "progressive" changes of the early Twentieth Century isn't the point here though. Rather, it seems that with the advent of corporate personhood and the resulting excesses of corporate greed, the vision of local community self government was largely lost to the hearts and minds of the people. They began to accept the notion that only the federal government was competent to solve modern problems. Thus, the establishment of corporate personhood worked as an engine of destruction, allowing ever greater power to be accumulated by corporations and dismantling the American system of local self government by making it seem irrelevant. This led directly to the next major blunder in the dismantling of the American system of government, the assumption of an unlimited federal authority over everything, which took place under the leadership of Franklin Roosevelt. This is the subject of the next chapter.

Footnotes:

1. *Unequal Protection: The Rise of Corporate Dominance and the Theft of Human Rights. (*Thom Hartmann, Rodale, 2004) p. 54-55

2. Ibid, p. 71

3. Ibid, p. 64

4. *The Anti Federalist Papers*, Ralph Ketcham, 1986, (Penguin Putnam Inc, 375 Hudson St., NY, NY, 10014), p.173

5. Ibid, p. 218

6. *Unequal Protection*, p.73

7. Ibid, p. 75-76

8. Ibid, p. 98

9. *Gangs of America*, Ted Nace, (Berrett-Koehler Publishers, Inc, San Francisco 2003), p.62

10. Ibid, p. 68-69

11. *Unequal Protection*, p. 88-89

12. Ibid, p. 121

13. Ibid, p. 157

14. Ibid, p. 107, 108

15. *Democracy in America*, Alexis de Tocqueville, J.P. Mayer-Ed., (Anchor Books, Garden City, NY 1969), P.179

16. *Jack London and His Times*, Joan London, 1939, (University of Washington Press American Library edition 1968), p. 307

17. *London- Novels and Social Writings*, Literary Classics of the United States, Inc., New York, NY 1982, P399-400

18. Ibid, p.405

19. Ibid, p.407-408

20. Ibid, P. 1162

21. *Democracy in America*, p. 68-69

Chapter 2

FDR and the End of Constitutionally Limited Government

"If the Constitution, intelligently and reasonably construed stands in the way of desirable legislation, the blame must rest upon that instrument, and not upon the court for enforcing it according to its terms. The remedy in that situation – and the only true remedy – is to amend the Constitution."

George Sutherland
U.S Supreme Court Justice in 1937

The second major blunder in the dismantling of the American republic was the wholesale subversion of constitutionally limited government under Franklin Roosevelt in the 1930s. The technical and constitutional violations perpetrated by Roosevelt will be looked at first, followed by an examination of the philosophical issues and the profound social and cultural decline ignited by following FDR's agenda.

Franklin Delano Roosevelt was elected President of the United States In November, 1932, and inaugurated as our 32nd President on March 4, 1933. On the day of his inauguration, banks were experiencing runs and closing their doors. It seemed that economic chaos was threatening to engulf the nation, as much of the economic structure erected during the Progressive era had started to unravel in 1929. Consequently, on March 9, 1933 President Roosevelt, after previously proclaiming a bank holiday and asking Congress to grant him powers equivalent to those of war, issued an emergency proclamation appropriating many of the powers under the

Trading with the Enemy Act of 1917. Using this authority, which basically suspended the Constitution, Roosevelt proceeded to seize privately held gold on April 5, 1933 and to advance the entire agenda of the New Deal from then on.

The prevailing national myth is that FDR came in at a moment of great crisis, and with bold, visionary leadership guided us out of the Great Depression and prevented us from going the way of Communism or Fascism. In the last decade or so, that myth has become doubtful and controversial, thanks to a couple of groundbreaking books, *The Forgotten Man, A New History of the Great Depression* by Amity Shlaes, (2007 HarperCollins Publishers) and *FDR's Folly*, by Jim Powell, (2003, Crown Forum)

These books make a compelling case that rather than shortening and easing the Great Depression, the New Deal policies of the Roosevelt administration actually lengthened and deepened it. Since a rehashing of all those economic policies is beyond the scope of this book, for the sake of credibility, let's consider the probable effects of just one aspect of those policies, the gold policy. It is hard to believe that the intrinsically unsettling actions of seizing all privately held gold bullion, taking the nation off the gold standard, and then just months later putting the nation back on the gold standard would create the kind of stable economic conditions attractive to investment, and therefore resulting in prosperity. FDR's administration took those actions, and they did not result in prosperity.

Since this book is looking at how our Constitution was taken from us, let's leave another critique of the New Deal economic failures to others, remembering only that Roosevelt used the ongoing economic crisis as a rationale to affect a multitude of political changes. The most important point is that far from saving us from the threat of Fascism, Franklin Roosevelt brought us into what amounts to a uniquely American form of fascism. The primary means used by Roosevelt to affect this change was that he negated the Tenth Amendment, and thereby ended the limited nature of the constitutionally limited republic framed by the founders.

The Tenth Amendment of the Constitution of the United States of America reads.

"The powers not delegated to the United States by the constitution, nor prohibited by it to the states, are reserved to the states respectively, or to the people."

This is the amendment that limited the powers of the federal, or as Thomas Jefferson termed it in his day, central government. The idea was that the states came together to form a government, and using a constitution, delegated to the central government certain limited powers. If over the course of time, we, as a nation, decided that the central or federal government should have more powers, we could amend the constitution to accomplish that end. For example, when we decided as a nation to prohibit alcohol, we enacted the Eighteenth Amendment, and when we decided that had been a bad idea, we enacted the Twenty-First Amendment, which repealed the Eighteenth Amendment. A little bit of a tedious process, but it ensures that the federal government is kept on a short leash, and that the people have a real say in deciding if federal powers will be increased.

This all changed under Franklin Delano Roosevelt. Using the aforementioned Emergency Proclamation of 1933, he proceeded to act as though the Tenth Amendment didn't exist, getting Congress to pass the "alphabet soup" of federal agencies in the first one hundred days of his administration. The constitutionality of many of the alphabet soup acts was questioned at the time and none more so than the National Recovery Act (NRA) which dictated, in minute detail, how small private companies must operate.

The constitutionality of the NRA was challenged in short order, but since the wheels of justice turn slowly, it wasn't until May 27, 1935 that the U.S. Supreme Court, in the Schechter case, ruled that the NRA was not constitutional. They made their ruling on the basis of the Tenth Amendment and on the fact that the commerce clause can't be stretched to give the federal government powers to regulate local businesses.

On May 31 of 1935, Franklin Roosevelt responded to the Supreme Court's decision with a press conference of unprecedented length and intensity. In it, and in the name of clarifying the situation so the public might understand the implications of the Court's ruling, FDR went into detail about how much the nation's economic interdependence had changed in the 150 years since the "horse and buggy" days when the Constitution was written. He also bemoaned the idea that this horse and buggy mentality would cause us to revert back to where the United States would be the only nation who's economic and social problems couldn't be solved by her national government using central planning. He ended with the promise that any new policy statements would be shortly forthcoming.

New policies certainly did come. Instead of taking the Court's thinking to heart, FDR forged ahead, effectively doubling down his bets. In the summer of 1935, knowing that the constitutionality of any new act would not be determined for years, FDR brought about the enactment of Social Security and passed some strongly pro-union laws. These were wildly popular, and ensured that he was re-elected by a landslide in 1936, allowing him to take advantage of huge majorities in both houses of Congress.

With his newly recharged political power, in March of 1937 FDR came out with his scheme to pack the Supreme Court to ensure that they would no longer find his policies unconstitutional. He proposed that Congress increase the number of justices on the Court so that he could ensure a majority agreed with him. At the same time, in the same "fireside chat" he dismissed the idea of amending the constitution as being too time consuming and indefinite. After all, justices could, in his view, read those words any way they chose, so why bother. With this scheme in the air, and with FDR having the political muscle to carry it out, the Supreme Court was intimidated into backing down, and approved his policies even though they never had conformed to constitutional guidelines.

It's been off to the races ever since, with a run away federal government having virtually no check on its ability to insert itself into any area of business or social programs. What's more, it's difficult to find many voices of opposition to what FDR did at the time, and that is probably due to two factors. First of all, it was a fait accompli; that is, since he had done it and gotten away with it, what use was there in disturbing everyone. Second, there was an ongoing financial crisis, in that FDR's economic policies had failed so badly that there was what has been called a depression within a depression in 1937. So in the name of national unity, most voices of opposition were muted by a triumphant President.

To find those voices of opposition, we must go back to the aftermath of the Schechter decision. The day after the Court's decision was handed down on May 28, 1935 the New York Times ran almost wall to wall coverage of the Shechter case and its implications for the NRA and indeed, the entire New Deal. In the same edition, they ran a sampling of opinion from other newspapers around the nation. Consider what these voices had to say at that moment.

From The Des Moines Register, "The high court has by unanimous vote demolished the pretty idea of just delegating to the President, or worse yet to industrial groups, large and undefined lawmaking powers over the economic life of the country. The Register has often made the point that this scheme was pure 'corporative stateism' of the kind Mussolini has given Italy. Too many things of too dubious value were done too impetuously and with too little regard for the Constitution back in 1933. The worst and foolishest was NRA."

From the Los Angeles Times, "The Supreme Court knocks the main foundation stone from under the whole structure of administration policy in its ruling that emergencies do not create constitutional powers and that Congress may not delegate to the President the right to do as he sees fit. Since it is on this plea that most of the New Deal processes of national regimentation have been predicated, the rulings devastatingly inclusive character is obvious. It makes abundantly clear that the days of a virtually uncontrolled one-man dictatorship in the United States are at an end."

From The St. Paul Pioneer Press, "The decision overthrowing practically all that is vital in the NIRA does far more than merely to invalidate the codes as they stand. It is really notice that the historic and fundamental division of powers between the State and the Federal governments cannot be revised by judicial rewriting of the Constitution. Liberals and conservatives on the bench alike agree that the Constitution does stand as a bulwark against usurpation by the Federal Government of the powers over business and industry which were regarded as the province of the states."

From The Kansas City Star, "The Constitution is supreme; it cannot be made to mean what it does not say or stretched to cover a broad and virtually unrestricted grant of power even in the name of an emergency. Aside from its constitutional phases, the experience with the operations of the National Industrial Recovery Act demonstrated that on the whole it has retarded recovery. But there were certain features of the codes that ought to be lived up to. Business would make a fatal mistake if it tried to take advantage of the decision to bring back sweat-shop conditions, throw men out of work and return to child labor."

From The Portland Oregonian, "The Supreme Court has re-established the fact that there is no room within the Constitution for centralized government. Its unanimity even disposes of the prospect that by reorganizing and liberalizing the court, safe conduct could be obtained around constitutional barriers for the power yearnings of young intellectuals of the administration. Attempt by new law to salvage anything from NRA wreckage would be but a forlorn, face saving enterprise. The reverberations of its collapse have shaken AAA, the Securities Bill, the Wagner Labor Disputes Act. 'Back to the Constitution' is no longer a forceful slogan. We are there."

From The Philadelphia Inquirer, "The Supreme Court here epitomizes representative government as it was envisioned by the founders. It establishes the truth that no matter what wrecking crew attempts to destroy the vitality of American principles, it must eventually face the highest legal authority for the ratification of its acts, so long as the Constitution is in force. If the wreckers want to change American doctrine, they must first annul the Constitution, not by indirection or evasion, but by common consent and lawful agreement."

Finally, even this entry from the New York Herald Tribune made its way onto the pages of the New York Times on this momentous day.

"The consequences of the NRA decision are unquestionably far-reaching. The demise of the Blue Eagle (the symbol of the NRA) is not exactly startling news- the President was about the only one left in Washington who refused to concede its failure and collapse. But the Wagner bill and the AAA amendments seem equally cast out by the logic of the decision. If the term interstate commerce is to be held to its clear meaning as consistently interpreted by the Supreme Court and as now reiterated, then all the clever phraseology by which the New Dealers are seeking to evade the Constitutional clause will be so much vain trickery. The AAA has yet to come before the Supreme Court, and, in so far as it depends upon voluntary cooperation by the individual farmer, it may survive. Yet the trick by which compulsion was applied to the cotton farmer seems a blatant evasion of the Constitution; and the whole device of a processing tax may ultimately go overboard.

"The course of the President remains to be decided. If he is candid and has been sincere in his radical policies he will seek the amendment of the Constitution to alter its basic structure and permit the socialization and regimentation of industry. Thereby would be raised an honest and straightforward issue which could be fought out on its merits. But the blow to the President's pride is heavy. The damage to his prestige is great. He is shown after two years, by the unanimous opinion of the Supreme Court, including all its most liberal and progressive members, to have been leading the country down a blind alley."

As mentioned, instead of taking some of this opposition to heart, Franklin Roosevelt doubled down on his strategy, pushing through Social Security and strongly pro-union legislation before the next presidential election in 1936. These long sought and popular reforms recharged the New Deal, handed FDR a landslide in the 1936 election at both the presidential and congressional contests, and allowed him to consider that he had a mandate to do whatever he wished.

Consider this excerpt from FDR's Second Inaugural Address, January 20, 1937. "We are beginning to wipe out the line that divides the practical from the ideal; and in so doing we are fashioning an instrument of unimagined power for the establishment of a morally better world." With the success of his court packing scheme, or rather with the way it intimidated the Supreme Court into ruling in his favor, Roosevelt was well on his way to establishing that "instrument of unimagined power".

Some did continue to fight a rear guard action against this change of government, as seen in the following passage from *FDR's Folly*.

"Every bit as important as the FDR Court's decisions upholding compulsory unionism were its decisions upholding Social Security. This, as already noted, involved taxing some people (younger workers) to benefit other people (those who retired), in violation of the general welfare clause, which had long been held to mean that taxpayers' money should be spent to benefit all the people, not particular individuals or factions. Justice Cardozo, writing the majority opinion in *Helvering v Davis*, 301 U.S. 619 (May 24, 1937), suggested the general welfare clause was meaningless, standing for one thing at one time and another thing at another time.

Justices McReynolds and Butler, dissenting from Helvering, countered by saying that the general welfare clause 'is not a substantive general power to provide for the welfare of the United States but is a limitation on the grant of power to raise money by taxes, duties, and imports.' The justices continued, 'If it were otherwise, all the rest of the Constitution, consisting of carefully enumerated and cautiously guarded grants of specific powers, would have been useless, if not delusive.'

Further, McReynolds and Butler were "of opinion that the provisions of the act here challenged are repugnant to the Tenth Amendment." They elaborated with separate dissenting opinions in a related Social Security case, *Steward Machine Co. v Collector of Internal Revenue*, 301 U.S. 548 (May 24, 1937). McReynolds expressed the enumerated powers principle when he wrote, 'I cannot find any authority in the Constitution for making the Federal Government the great almoner of public charity throughout the United States...Can it be controverted that the great mass of the business of Government- that involved in the social relations, the internal arrangements of the body politic, the mental and moral culture of men, the development of local resources of wealth, the punishment of crimes in general, the preservation of order, the relief of the needy or otherwise unfortunate members of society- did in practice remain with the States; that none of these objects of local concern are by the Constitution expressly or impliedly prohibited to the States, and that none of them are by any express language of the Constitution transferred to the United States? Can it be claimed that any of these functions of local administration and legislation are vested in the Federal Government by any implication? I have never found anything in the Constitution which is susceptible of such a construction. No one of the enumerated powers touches the subject, or has even a remote analogy to it.'"[1]

Also in *FDR's Folly*, the following passage quoted from Roger Pilon sums up what happened, in spite of and contrary to the wisdom of Justice McReynolds, and how we find ourselves in our present dilemma,

"In a nutshell, a document of delegated, enumerated, and thus limited powers became in short order a document of effectively unenumerated powers, limited only by rights that would thereafter be interpreted narrowly by conservatives on the Court and episodically by liberals on the Court. Both sides, in short, would come to ignore our roots in limited government, buying instead into the idea of vast majoritarian power – the only disagreement being over what rights might limit that power and in which circumstances." [2]

To reinforce that last point, that both sides (big business and big government types) embraced these changes, consider that in the next presidential election, that of 1940, Wendell

Willkie gave Roosevelt a run for his money, but lost in the end. As a big business man, a developer of interstate utilities, and a recently former Democrat, it is easy to believe that Willkie would have continued the policies of federal control of industry and the economy.

There is some powerful evidence to this effect as well. On July 15, 1940, in the newsletter "In Fact", George Seldes revealed the following about what Willkie had said: "1. In an address to the National Press Club in Washington Willkie spoke openly for industrial dictatorship in the United States. [I explained to readers that this approximated Mussolini's corporate totalitarian state]" [3]

He would probably have thought that while some of the federal regulations can be irksome, nonetheless when business is conducted at the federal, as opposed to the state level, it is always, at least in theory, more efficient and cost effective. There is only one set of legislators that must be lobbied, after all. So from the vantage point of the late 1930's, we can see the fully evolved fascist beast emerging from its shell. Both the believers in centralized government and the believers in centralized business were happy to see its birth, and though they thought they were working against each other, collectively they were working to nurture its growth. There will be more about this shortly.

The dire philosophical consequence of these changes becomes clear when we resort to the thoughts of the esteemed Thomas Jefferson recorded in a couple of private letters to friends. "Our country is too large to have all its affairs directed by a single government. Public servants at such a distance, and from under the eye of their constituents, must, from the circumstance of distance, be unable to administer and overlook all the details necessary for the good government of the citizens, and the same circumstance, by rendering detection impossible to their constituents, will invite the public agents to corruption, plunder, and waste. And I do verily believe, that if the principle were to prevail, of a common law being in force in the United States..., it would become the most corrupt government on the earth..." This is from a letter to Gideon Granger, 1800. [4]

In the same vein in another letter to William T. Barry, 1822, Jefferson wrote, "If ever this vast country is brought under a single government, it will be one of the most extensive corruption." [5]

Perhaps in echo to Jefferson, another great student of democratic republican government laid out his thoughts. In *Democracy In America,* Alexis de Tocqueville wrote,

"However, the strength of free peoples resides in the local community. Local institutions are to liberty what primary schools are to science; they put it within the people's reach, they teach people to appreciate its peaceful enjoyment and accustom them to make use of it. Without local institutions a nation may give itself a free government, but it has not got the spirit of liberty. Passing passions, momentary interest, or chance circumstances may give it the external shape of independence, but the despotic tendencies which have been driven into the interior of the body social will sooner or later break out on the surface." [6]

Ignoring Tocqueville's warning, Franklin Roosevelt took almost all real power from the municipalities, the towns, communities, and states, and put them all in the hands of a distant federal government. In doing so, he sowed the ground for a near collapse of the spirit of community and self government.

It is important, while the discussion is focused on the philosophical flaws in Roosevelt's thinking, to bring up an important slight aside. While "Fascism" is an apt description of FDR'ism, used against him in many of the already quoted newspaper editorials, "Fascism" remains a confusing, emotionally charged word

Consequently, some background about "Fascism" is in order. The best, and classic, definition of Fascism says it is a combination of the forces of big business together with the forces of big government operating against the interests of the poor, working and entrepreneurial classes, and using the tools of science to control the minds and culture of the people.

Let's go a little deeper to understand this definition. Mussolini and the Fascists rose in Italy in the early Twentieth Century as an offshoot of Marxism. Basically, the Fascisti (a term derived from the idea of bundling, standardizing and collectivizing) called for a form of Marxism that would leave much of the small business economy alone, and collectivize only the major industries, or in Marxist parlance, the major means of production. In addition, Mussolini introduced the idea that this new form of Marxism should be advanced by using modern science to mold the minds and the culture of the masses, to as he termed it, be a totalitarian government, designed to control the total life of the populace.

That basic concept of Fascism was changed during World War Two, when the tail of government found itself not capable of wagging the dog of the major capitalists, and the relationship reverted back to its historic arrangement with big money directing the government's policies for the good of the upper classes. They nonetheless retained the Fascist image of populism and its tools of cultural molding and mind control. In other words, the business and political elites joined together to rule over the masses like little despots. That's what fascism has become in the modern real world.

This small-f fascism is one, not of a particular political party, but rather it is the most accurate description of the real kind of government America has had for the last seventy years or so. The way this American fascism has grown has not been so much a smooth creeping as a ratcheting between the big business party, and the big government party, mostly at the times of presidential elections. Think of the following in terms of the transition to Kennedy from the Republicans in 1960, Nixon from the Democrats in 1968, Carter from the Republicans in 1976, Reagan from the Democrats, Clinton from the Republicans, Bush from the Democrats, and Obama from the Republicans.

Say the Republicans are in power, giving the store away to the big business greedhead types. We get sick of it, and the Democrats say "elect us and we'll roll back the excesses of big business". So we elect them, and we are perennially disappointed when they mightily increase the amount of government regulation and involvement with our personal lives and don't manage to beat back corporate greed a bit (it might even get a little worse).

Then, every four to eight years or so, after we are getting sick of the new governmental controls, the Republicans say, "elect us and we'll get government off your backs". So we elect them, and they concentrate on increasing corporate profits and making sure that the already wealthy get even wealthier. Big government intrusion into and regulation over our lives diminishes not a whit, but in fact grows a little. Then, after we once again get sick of the runaway greed, along come the Democrats, repeating their promise of, "elect us and we'll roll back the excesses of big business".

And so it goes, on and on, back and forth, left and right. At each election, there is a seemingly permanent national division around the issues of morality, peace, justice and the like. These issues, which should mostly be settled between neighbors in community, (more on this in coming chapters) have been nationalized by dubious court rulings or non rulings. Consequently, those of us who care about them almost all feel compelled to vote for one side of the dichotomy or the other. Then, when elected, the authorities of either party deliver just enough on the issues we care about to keep us passionately divided from our neighbors, and for the rest of their term advance the fascist agenda of more power and money to big business and big government.

Every one of these times of change acts like a social/ political ratchet, a sudden change that moves only in one direction, and stops at a new political equilibrium for a few years. At every move of the ratchet, toward big business or big government, the combined centralizing forces of big business and big government gain increasing power over our lives.

This is why it is accurate to call modern America a fascist country, because even though "Fascism" isn't in the platforms of either major political party, the real world results of the interplay of the actions of both parties, when considered together, has tended to centralize and combine the powers of big government with the powers of big business, and use them to act against the interests of the working, entrepreneurial, and poor classes.

In addition, the aspect that makes this system distinct from old fashioned "despotism" is that the political and economic power over us is used, ala classic fascism, to shape our minds and culture. This involves the education system, the media, corporate advertising, and any number of culture changing court decisions. Mussolini originally proposed using the power of modern media and psychology to mold the minds of the people. The idea was that humanity could be perfected by the strict enforcement of well conceived laws and the use of modern technology to mold minds.

This can be seen in action in all the schools of fascism, from the Hitler youth of the Nazis to the Young Pioneers and Cultural Revolutions of the Marxists in China and Russia, to the social engineering advanced by the educators and social workers in the liberal welfare state started by FDR. (The assertion here, which will be expanded on later, is that fascism is at the center of all the "isms", and that communism, socialism,

Nazism, and FDR'ism are all, when seen in light of being combinations of the power of the state with big capital against the people, just schools of fascism.)

So first we must realize that "Fascism" means a combination of big business and big government operating against the interests of the poor, working and entrepreneurial classes which also uses modern science to mold the hearts and minds of the people. Then we can see that a fascist oligarchy is certainly what we have today in America. For that matter, a similar power structure is taking rule over most of the planet; a growing and terrifying international fascist oligarchy.

After that aside, let's return to the main narrative. Franklin Roosevelt considered that he was "fashioning an instrument of unimagined power for the establishment of a morally better world" and that to do so the nation must, in Jefferson's terms, be "brought under a single government," even though in doing so, "it will be one of the most extensive corruption." This bringing of the nation under a single, federal law was the first of Franklin Roosevelt's three major mistakes.

FDR's second major mistake was the methodology he employed to bring about this change to our constitutional system of government. In short, he cheated. Instead of forthrightly using constitutional procedures to get the changes he wanted, which many people were suggesting, he used demagoguery and power politics to in effect repeal the Tenth Amendment. "If the Constitution, intelligently and reasonably construed," wrote Supreme Court Justice Sutherland in 1937, "stands in the way of desirable legislation, the blame must rest upon that instrument, and not upon the court for enforcing it according to its terms. The remedy in that situation – and the only true remedy – is to amend the Constitution." [7]

To understand how profoundly Roosevelt betrayed the cause of American constitutional government, and indeed the cause of self government around the world, we will look more closely at his "Fireside Chat" of March 9, 1937, his "Court Packing Scheme" chat, which can be found on the Internet.

"I want—as all Americans want—an independent judiciary as proposed by the framers of the Constitution. That means a Supreme Court that will enforce the Constitution as written, that will refuse to amend the Constitution by the arbitrary exercise of judicial power—in other words by judicial say-so. It does not mean a judiciary so independent that it can deny the existence of facts which are universally recognized.

"How then could we proceed to perform the mandate given us? It was said in last year's Democratic platform, and here are the words, "if these problems cannot be effectively solved within the Constitution, we shall seek such clarifying amendments as will assure the power to enact those laws, adequately to regulate commerce, protect public health and safety, and safeguard economic security." In their words, we said we would seek an amendment only if every other possible means by legislation were to fail.

"When I commenced to review the situation with the problem squarely before me, I came by a process of elimination to the conclusion that, short of amendments, the only method which was clearly constitutional, and would at the same time carry out other much needed reforms, was to infuse new blood into all our courts."

He then went on to detail his scheme to appoint a new justice to the court for every justice over seventy who refused to retire. And he assured his audience about the new justices.

"If by that phrase "packing the Court" it is charged that I wish to place on the bench spineless puppets who would disregard the law and would decide specific cases as I wished them to be decided, I make this answer: that no president fit for his office would appoint, and no Senate of honorable men fit for their office would confirm, that kind of appointees to the Supreme Court.

"But if by that phrase the charge is made that I would appoint and the Senate would confirm justices worthy to sit beside present members of the Court, who understand modern conditions, that I will appoint justices who will not undertake to override the judgment of the Congress on legislative policy, that I will appoint justices who will act as justices and not as legislators—if the appointment of such justices can be called 'packing the Courts,' then I say that I and with me the vast majority of the American people favor doing just that thing-now."

So he didn't want puppets, just justices who would agree with his assessment of "modern conditions", and help to advance his goal of "fashioning an instrument of unimagined power for the establishment of a morally better world". How high minded of him.

So why didn't he just do as many, even in his own party, urged him to do, and use his vast political clout to amend the constitution to his liking? Let's consider his reasons from the same fireside chat.

"There are many types of amendment proposed. Each one is radically different from the other. But there is no substantial group within the Congress or outside the Congress who are agreed on any single amendment.

"I believe that it would take months or years to get substantial agreement upon the type and language of an amendment. It would take months and years thereafter to get a two-thirds majority in favor of that amendment in both houses of the Congress.

"Then would come the long course of ratification by three-quarters of all the states. No amendment which any powerful economic interests or the leaders of any powerful political party have had reason to oppose has ever been ratified within anything approaching a reasonable time. And remember that thirteen states which contain only five percent of the voting population can block ratification even though the thirty-five states with ninety-five percent of the population are in favor of it.

A very large percentage of newspaper publishers and chambers of commerce and bar associations and manufacturers' associations, who are trying to give the impression today that they really do want a constitutional amendment, would be the very first to exclaim as soon as an amendment was proposed, "Oh! I was for an amendment all right, but this amendment that you've proposed is not the kind of an amendment that I was thinking about. And so, I am going to spend my time, my efforts, and my money to block this amendment, although I would be awfully glad to help to get some other kind of an amendment ratified."

Two groups oppose my plan on the ground that they favor a constitutional amendment. The first includes those who fundamentally object to social and economic legislation along modern lines. This is the same group who, during the recent campaign, tried to block the mandate of the people. And the strategy of that last stand is to suggest the time-consuming process of amendment in order to kill off by delay the legislation demanded by the mandated. To those people I say, I do not think you will be able long to fool the American people as to your purposes.

The other group is composed of those who honestly believe the amendment process is the best and who would be willing to support a reasonable amendment if they could agree on one.

To them I say, we cannot rely on an amendment as the immediate or only answer to our present difficulties. When the time comes for action, you will find that many of those who pretend to support you will sabotage any constructive amendment which is proposed. Look at these strange bedfellows of yours. When before have you found them really at your side in your fights for progress?

And remember one thing more. Even if an amendment were passed and even if in the years to come it were to be ratified, its interpretation would depend upon the kind of justices who would be sitting on the Supreme Court bench. For an amendment, like the rest of the Constitution, is what the justices say it is rather than what its framers or you might hope it is."

So let's get this straight (and remember, this "chat" is the point in history when we, as a nation, abandoned the Constitution). First of all, Roosevelt asserts that there is no time for an amendment, because of it must be supposed, some kind of ongoing "crisis"? So, have his policies failed, after four years? And since he intended to ignore the Tenth Amendment from his first day in office, why didn't he propose its repeal then? By 1937, if the nation had agreed with him, it would have been a done deal.

More to the point, since there were so many different amendments being talked about, why didn't he forthrightly propose the repeal of the Tenth Amendment in 1937, and use his powers of leadership and the national consensus he claimed to get it accomplished. Even though the Supreme Court has occasionally handed down some questionable readings of the Constitution, repealing the Tenth Amendment, with the raging debate that would have caused, would have carried such clear meaning that the Court would have had no room to wiggle out of it.

So FDR could have proposed an amendment, repealing the Tenth Amendment, which would have been clearly understood by all as legitimating the entire New Deal. What's more, he was being disingenuous in the extreme when he claimed passage and ratification of such an amendment would take years. If the vast majority of the people were in favor of such an amendment, as he claimed and which might have been the case, then the entire process would have required no more time that had been taken for the Twenty-First Amendment, (repealing the Eighteenth Amendment prohibiting alcohol) which FDR first proposed early in 1933, and which had gained approval from two-thirds of both houses of congress, and ratification after being approved by three-fourths of the state's legislatures before 1933 was over.

He probably could have gotten that done, and even though he still would have blundered into the dangers of an over centralized government, at least we as a nation would know how we got to where we are today. Consider this snippet again, from the New York Herald Tribune, reprinted in the New York Times, May 28, 1935. "If he (President Roosevelt) is candid and has been sincere in his radical policies he will seek the amendment of the Constitution to alter its basic structure and permit the socialization and regimentation of industry. Thereby would be raised an honest and straightforward issue which could be fought out on its merits."

Of course, to give a cynical interpretation to the affair, FDR might not have been sure he could have such an amendment ratified, and knew that if the question were raised in a forthright way and lost, that he would not have been allowed to accomplish the same goals in the underhanded way that he did.

What's more, his circumvention of proper constitutional process might have had a more sinister motivation. It might have been a manifestation of a desire to free himself, and future presidents, from the burden of having to dot every "i" and cross every "t" of a "horse and buggy" constitution.

In making this second blunder, FDR deprived the nation, and generations of Americans who would follow, the right and power to make clear decisions about the course of the nation. We never had that debate about giving unlimited power to the federal government. FDR just took it, leaving us to wonder what had gone wrong with the system established by the founders.

The last paragraph quoted from his "chat" is the most disturbing, because he is revealed to have a deep contempt for not only the amendment process, but also for the concept of rule of law. "And remember one thing more. Even if an amendment were passed and even if in the years to come it were to be ratified, its meaning would depend upon the kind of justices who would be sitting on the Supreme Court bench. For an amendment, like the rest of the Constitution, is what the justices say it is rather than what its framers or you might hope it is."

To understand why this second blunder was so destructive to the American republic, we have to regain a deeper appreciation of the importance of the rule of law. To modern ears, emphasizing the rule of law sounds like a vaguely authoritarian obsession, as though the people must be forced to comply on every point. Actually, nothing could be further from the truth. The rule of law is the great defense the people have against being ruled over by oppressors. Essentially, we can either have the rule of law, or we will have the rule of the rich and powerful. The rule of law is the real connection the people have with their government.

Think about the connection of the people with government. They can vote for representatives, senators, governors, and the like, but that is only a small part of government. The real power is in the law. When we, as groups or individuals, want to change things, we go to our representatives, etc. and convince them to introduce legislation to change the law. In some states, we can initiate petitions, and get referendums put on the ballots for direct voting. In either case, we fight, struggle and argue to change the words that are written in the law. Then, once the battle is over, and we have succeeded in changing the law, we certainly expect the rule of law to prevail. We expect enforcement of new law. So the vital connection necessary for the efforts of the citizens to make any sense is that the law will be enforced as written.

When the nation was young, and the Constitution with its first ten amendments was being fought over, the people battled (with words, not swords) mightily with each other so that the final words written in the founding document and its first ten amendments reflected, as truly as possible, the will of the people. They expected that the words written to be followed as closely as humanly possible. They made provisions for changing the foundational document, as times dictated, by including a process for amending it.

But FDR says that because some justices might twist the meaning of words, let's abandon the constitutional processes altogether and rely on majoritarian power politics instead. He might be making a good case for impeaching a justice or two if they ignore the clear meanings of words, but not for causing the nation to decline into the kind of run away democracy the founders feared.

What's more, since that time, many of Roosevelt's apologists have insisted that we have a "living" Constitution. But since they ignore the living aspects established in the amendment process, what they mean is that the words written there mean whatever those in power can twist them into meaning, as FDR did. Now they can pick and choose whatever they want of the Constitution, and ignore whatever is inconvenient. While this certainly allows for a very powerful and activist government, which is the advantage of all despotic governments, it does so by severing almost all sense of connection to the government felt by the common person.

When the average American picks up the Constitution, s/he can barely recognize the government it defines as the government which rules over us. When we try to discern how we might fix the nation, it looks so confusing and hopeless that we decide to leave governing to the "politicians". Unfortunately, this is just what a despot would want us to do.

So in one long strategy carried out through the Great Depression, Franklin Roosevelt foisted two terrible mistakes on the American people. First of all, he centralized government to an extent never imagined by any of the founders, and that was warned against by the best of them. Second, he accomplished this dubious goal by ignoring and circumventing the Constitution itself, in violation of his oath of office. In sum, he delivered us up to an all powerful government, and went a long way toward eroding any sense of citizenship in the hearts and minds of the people. To describe him as a fascist and a traitor might seem very harsh, but it is probably the only truthful and accurate way to categorize him.

In his defense, he undoubtedly did not see himself in that way, but was probably driven by a tragic impatience, eager to bring the advantages of modern technological advances to the masses. This was a grave error as his impatience was unwarranted. While the processes and debates of free people governing themselves can be very messy (a lot like making sausage) and appear to consume too much valuable time; in the end a free people will almost always choose the best path.

Take, for instance, the case of the Tennessee Valley Authority, one of the linchpins of the New Deal. It was a system of dams and hydroelectric plants to prevent floods and electrify the rural South. It accomplished some of that, but private enterprise did as much and more in the same neighborhood.

In *FDR's Folly* discussing how the Tennessee Valley Authority actually slowed the electrification of the rural south, Palmer writes,

"Ironically, The Tennessee Valley actually lagged other regions in electrification, even though David Lilienthal aggressively promoted electricity and electrical appliances. As Chandler explained, 'Rural electrification did not proceed as rapidly in the TVA area as elsewhere nearby. In 1930 Tennessee held a slight advantage over Georgia. About 4 percent of Tennessee's and 3 percent of Georgia's farms had power, compared to 13 percent nationwide... By 1940 Tennessee trailed Georgia in rural electrification...All major TVA states trailed North Carolina, Virginia, and Georgia.'

Why were people in the TVA region slower to adopt electricity? Chandler explained that use of electricity correlated with income. The more money people earned, the more electrical appliances they could afford, and the more electricity they would tend to use. To the degree that the TVA slowed the rate of progress, by subsidizing people in existing, low-paying farm work and reducing their incentive to find higher-paying work elsewhere, the TVA undermined a fundamental factor in the demand for electricity." [8]

FDR's impatience and his subverting of the Constitution to get the advantages of the Industrial Revolution to the people as quickly as possible actually slowed that progress compared to allowing free market forces to operate. If it were possible to make similar comparisons of FDR's other social and economic policies with areas that didn't fall under his policies, we have to suspect that his centralized government approach will usually be found to be inferior to a decentralized, free, local self government approach. In most cases though, since the federal writ ran over the entire nation, such comparisons can't be made.

Social Security

While the constitutional violations and usurpations of the Roosevelt era are an overwhelming problem unto themselves, there is an even larger problem, at least as far as those of us who wish to revive free self government are concerned. FDR's third mistake is that some of the most revered aspects of the New Deal have so greatly eroded the morals and culture of the people, that we have virtually been rendered incapable of self government. The most important of these morally degrading programs is the so called untouchable third rail of American politics; Social Security.

Social Security, the most holy of all holy cows, will now be soberly examined and questioned. This is certainly not to frighten those dependent on this program. We must make a solemn commitment that we will not fundamentally alter the system without ensuring a painless transition to those already in the system. Even if we decide to totally end Social Security, human compassion demands that we not pull the rug out from under those already dependent upon it. If there is a dismantling, it will be a compassionate, phased dismantling. Consequently, no one should try to prevent this discussion out of fear for their own personal security, or the security of the helpless and elderly.

Nonetheless, we simply must have the discussion because Social Security has been, without most people realizing it, the driving force behind the massive social decline of this nation. Moreover, a close scrutiny of Social Security will open our eyes to the insidious anti-community, anti-family effects of the entire federal socialistic structure, and how that "liberal" structure is inevitably totalitarian and doomed to collapse under the weight of its own internal contradictions

It will surprise many to realize that the most important problems created by Social Security have to do not with the financial stability of the system, although that is a problem, but rather with the morality and education of our young. Consider the world before Social Security. The fact that there was no Social Security or Medicare to fall back on made people's thinking about old age far different from today's. People worked hard and saved their money for their declining years, much like today. But those individual savings wouldn't have been enough to ensure peace of mind, as they aren't enough today. Through the ages, the life savings of the working and middle classes have been eaten up by any number of causes i.e., economic depressions, hyperinflation, natural disasters, and catastrophic illness. Consequently, people have always felt a need for more security than can be provided by personal savings. Before Social Security, that need was met by strong communities and even stronger families.

In the old way, (which held sway before the 1930's back through time to the mists of pre-history) before Social Security, there were a number of conclusions that almost everyone came to about how to deal with old age. In fact, people didn't so much reach these conclusions as inherit them, because they were the same common sense ways that had been practiced by their parents and grandparents.

One of the conclusions was to have large families. Large families were common back in those days. Of course, there were religious reasons, but they concurred with the wisdom of the people. It was thought that out of a large family, one or two of the children would make good, and help the others get set up in life as well as provide for the parents in their old age, if needed. The change in thinking about the size of families will be touched on again in this chapter, as it is the prime reason the system is going broke.

Another unspoken conclusion was that of character formation. Before Social Security, the parents had a vested interest in the character of their children. There were no government entitlements, and the family was the provider of last resort. People took a lot more care about the character of their children, because they had a lot more to lose if their children had poor character. If a child was allowed to grow up being selfish, a bully, or in other ways immoral, the parents could expect little help even if the child became rich. On the other hand, if the children were allowed to grow up lazy, or not capable of making their way in the world, that would also jeopardize the security and happiness of the parent's old age.

To be sure, very few families thought these things out in a conscious way. It's just the way things were done. Additionally, the community exerted a lot of pressure to keep things that way. The community was made up of many families operating under the same conclusions. If a child went “bad”, it was a reflection on the whole family, and the parents were expected to fix the problem. In that way, the lines of accountability and responsibility were maintained throughout the community. These lines carried great authority because the community/family, not the federal government, was the provider of last resort.

In the old days, parents put a lot of effort into forming the character of their children, ensuring that they were both competent and moral. This wasn't just because they loved their children, but because they saw that their future security might depend on the level of their children's character. It may sound like they were very selfish and calculating. They weren't. It's just that human beings will always be human, and human nature, like electricity, will always follow the path of least resistance.

If the only way a person can feel secure about growing old is to invest time and energy into the community and into the character of their children that is what a person will do. On the other hand, if the only thing a person has to do to feel comfortable about growing old is to maintain a relationship with the federal government, then that is all the average person will do.

It's not that parents don't love their children today, since the advent of Social Security, it's just that raising children can be difficult. From sleepless nights, to changing diapers, all the diseases, the teenage years, raising children is very draining, even to the worst and most uncaring of parents. To the best of parents, it's a full time vocation.

At every stage of the process, at every crisis, minor or major, there is a temptation on the part of the parent to say "so what." It's easy to slip into a mode of just doing enough to keep the chaos at bay, or to keep social services from the door, but not going deep enough to solve the character problems that are beginning to appear. Even though we can see that the child will be a weaker adult because of correctable character flaws, many of us fail to address the problems. It is easier on the parent and many think, "The problem doesn't really threaten me while the little snot is a child, and at 18 they're out'a here. What they do after that is their business, and none of mine."

Social Security attacks the family by greatly reducing the vested interest parents have in the character of their children. In that way, Social Security acts like a corrosive social poison, changing society at the molecular level of the nuclear family, profoundly affecting the relationship between parents and their children.

Of course, not every family has fallen for the bait. There are many families still focused on character development, but Social Security has encouraged the tendency to ignore it. This has created a kind of social wind of peer pressure which is very difficult for parents who do want to raise strong and good children to stand against. Undoubtedly, some parents succeed, but it is undeniable that many families are failing.

There are a couple of phenomena that can be pointed to as evidence that Social Security is having this effect on our culture. One is what was named the "generation gap," the split between the cultures of the young and the old. It was first noted as a real problem in the 1960's, and has gotten worse ever since. It came about when the first generation to be raised under the culture of Social Security, those born in the 1920's and 30's were raising their own children. The first generation raised with Social Security in its future wasn't overly concerned when its young, for the first time, developed a distinct and hostile culture. There has always been some friction between young and old, but nothing like the ongoing youth rebellion that started in the 1960's existed before then.

Another piece of evidence is the work and popularity of Dr. Spock. In the 1950's and 60's he advocated that we should basically let children raise themselves, not inflict our discipline on them, and they would be happier and healthier. These concepts first became popular among the first generation of parents growing up with Social Security in their future. These ideas first started making sense within the matrix of a Social Security culture.

Eroding parental priorities is the most powerful and insidious aspect of Social Security. By toppling the ancient regime of the family, Social Security changes the entire framework within which we conduct our culture. It changes the thinking of every man, loosening his relationships with everyone else, except the relationship with the federal government. Consequently, Social Security, in working as an insidious poison on the foundational cell of the nuclear family, weakens the whole living body of society.

What's more, since there are now so many dependent on Social Security, it can accurately be considered a social addiction. When thinking about how Social Security affects our nation, and why it must be stopped, it will be accurate to think of it as an addictive, corrosive, social poison.

We can now see how the erosion of family and community thinking caused by Social Security has worked hand in glove with the socialistic thinking that erected the whole federal socialist structure. Once the individual is no longer dependent on or strongly connected with family and community, there isn't much of a reason to defend the prerogatives of local community, nor to seek community based solutions to the problems that arise.

When a federal "solution" is proposed, we are quick to agree to it because it conforms to our prejudice that local community is irrelevant and probably incompetent. Besides, giving it to the federal government to fix allows us to go on with our private lives not having to take the time and energy required to actually solve civic problems.

Take, for example, the problems of teen gangs and teen pregnancy. The community way of dealing with these problems, the old fashioned way, would be with meetings, activism, and social pressure. The community as a whole would put pressure on the kids and the families to change their behavior. If simple persuasion didn't work, they could resort to the tools of boycott, ostracism, and stigmatizing of the offending parties. The families, parents, aunts, uncles and grandparents, would respond to this community pressure because, to ignore it might threaten their prestige in the community, their livelihood, and their entire material security. The kids, in their turn, would respond to familial pressure because the family, and not the federal government, was the provider of last resort.

That's not how it works today. Community pressure can't be brought to bear, because no one is dependent on the community. Consequently, that approach is rarely tried. Instead, when some sort of social problem appears, we immediately throw up our hands, abandoning a community approach, and call for a new federal program.

Is medical care needed for the poor and elderly? Instead of organizing local, low cost clinics, we call for a federal program. Is environmental pollution a problem? Instead of boycotting the offending corporations (or threatening to pull their charters), we call for a federal program. Is education a problem? Instead of dealing with our failing school systems with unrelenting passion born of the fact that the morality and competence of our children figures so large in our future lives, we passively look to the federal government for programs like No Child Left Behind. Throughout this whole process, the fact that we are operating in the matrix of a Social Security based culture causes our attempts at solutions to exacerbate, and not solve, the underlying problems.

What's more, this is where we can see the inevitable totalitarian nature of socialism in general. Solutions to social problems that depend on distant government weaken community and erode personal moral virtues. This creates more social problems that if dealt with, again by distant government programs, further weakens community and further erodes personal moral virtue. This vicious cycle will end with either social collapse or a totalitarian government; the horrific choice of abandoning civilization, or adopting draconian police state measures. In either case, we move away from being a free people.

Obviously, this analysis of American moral decline is oversimplified and generalized. There are many other factors, in addition to Social Security and socialism in general, which have contributed to the decline of family and community. Mass culture, movies, music, and television especially, have worked to break down the insularity of local communities. Mobility, in the form of planes and cars, has greatly increased the geographical range of the average person, and in so doing exposed us to many different ways of doing things. There are many other factors, the arts, the wars, the easing of travel restrictions between nations, and many unmentioned others, which have impelled a breakdown of community spirit while at the same time encouraging a powerful cosmopolitanism.

What's more (and it might shock some to see this admitted) a lot of this cosmopolitan spirit has been good. An increase in tolerance and an appreciation of the contributions made by all cultures is a fresh and hopefully abiding advance made by this era of Americans. However, the increase in cosmopolitan appreciation need not come at the expense of losing our precious community spirit.

Social Security (and the welfare state that has accompanied it) has been the unnoticed, unheralded, and yet leading cause of the breakdown in community. The insidious, corrosive aspect of Social Security (the Social Security matrix) so changes the basic assumptions of the individual, that it is appropriate to refer to pre and post Social Security thinking.

In the post Social Security world, there isn't an immediate breakdown in community and family. With the existence of Social Security, the individual no longer has much of a reason to exert the effort it will take to ensure a strong and moral community and family. In the long run, that factor alone will cause an erosion of family and community. Add to that modern technology, (and the fact that all the modern technology has been seen through the lens of, digested and used by the mind of a post- Social Security society) and the process accelerates. Combine that with a post Social Security peer pressure which denies any kind of objective moral truth, and community consensus is impossible. Finally, throw in some sort of federal socialistic scheme every time there is a problem caused by breakdown of family or community, further taking the power from community, further encouraging and enabling a moral decline which increases the negative synergy, and the pace of the breakdown accelerates to a confusing blur. As asserted, social breakdown or totalitarian government looms as the only two realistic alternative futures.

Another of the internal contradictions of centralized socialism is the fact that Social Security is going broke. Although the estimates of when the next crisis in Social Security financing will occur vary from ten to twenty-five years, everyone agrees that there will be a crisis.

The inevitability of the crisis stems from two factors. First, the percentage of the population receiving Social Security benefits is increasing every year, and will continue to increase at a dramatic rate into the foreseeable future. This is due to the huge numbers of people in the baby boom generation beginning their retirement years. The second factor is that the percentage of the population paying into the system is declining due to people having smaller families in the last fifty or so years.

The combination of these two factors will result in a diminishment of already meager benefits, and an increase in already high taxes withheld from income. Even with those changes, the day will come when the revenue available won't cover the benefits people need. The system will be broke. No one knows what will happen then, but when it happens, it won't be pretty.

The problem arises because Social Security isn't a pension fund, where people pay into a fund, and then receive payments from their investment when they are old. The people receiving benefits today are being paid with money from the income of people working today. So it's basically just a pyramid scheme where today's workers are sending money to the people at the top of the list (retirees) with the hope that no one will break the chain and their benefits will be there when they need them.

The problem is that like any pyramid scheme, Social Security requires that there be many more people at the bottom of the pyramid than at the top. With baby boomer retirement, and the small modern nuclear family, the demographics no longer look like a pyramid, but instead, they resemble a top heavy column with fewer people on the bottom than the top.

When Social Security was first conceived, this would never have been a problem, because in those days people had large families. The irony is that, as previously noted, the reason folks in the past had large families was having a lot of children was a form of old age insurance

This then is another of the internal contradictions of centralized socialism. Social Security won't work unless people have large families, and yet people aren't motivated to have large families because Social Security exists. There needs to be a broad base on the pyramid. The nature of this particular pyramid destroys any reason for individuals to broaden the base.

Finally, the last major internal contradiction built into the socialistic structure foisted on us by the administration of Franklin Delano Roosevelt is also the one that should give us the most hope these mistakes can be reversed. Virtually every program that endures from the New Deal was established by ignoring the words written in the Constitution. This is an especially awkward problem, because these programs allow federal bureaucrats to insert their rules and regulations, which must be followed to the minutest letter, into the most intimate places of our lives. Yet the authority for doing so rests on a laughably loose and incoherent reading of the basic law of the land. Thus, we have arrived at a system of lawful lawlessness, or unlawful legalisms. If we were to apply the laws and regulations of the left with the same (living) misuse of language with which they treat the Constitution, we could do anything we want. On the other hand, if they used the words of the Constitution with the same strict adherence that they expect for their "laws", they wouldn't have the power that they do today.

To summarize this chapter, Franklin Delano Roosevelt accomplished the second major blunder in the dismantling of the American Republic, the wholesale abandonment of constitutionally limited government. He did it in an underhanded way that greatly diminished the connection of the citizens to their government, and to their responsibilities as free citizens. What's more, some of the fascist agenda that he enacted has worked like an addictive, corrosive social poison that has rendered the American people almost incapable of community self government. Now, we are seemingly destined for either social collapse or totalitarian despotism.

Earlier, FDR was described as being a fascist traitor. While that description is probably accurate, he certainly didn't intend to play that role, nor did he see himself as such. Actually, in a moment of candor at the beginning of his reign as President, he might well have admitted an admiration for the ideas of Mussolini and the Fascists. Many did approve of what Mussolini did at first, and they all admitted that "He made the trains run on time." Later on, after we went to war against him, and the excesses of strong man rule became obvious, most of his earlier admirers turned away. They still liked the basic ideas of Fascism, and so they (and FDR must be included in their number) remained essentially fascists.

The more problematic accusation is that Franklin Roosevelt betrayed not only the American Republic, but the cause of constitutional self government worldwide. He did this, changing the role of the federal government from one of limited enumerated powers to one of unlimited powers to be used however the Congress and the President saw fit, and he made this change without the use of the constitutional amendment process available to him.

The second part of Roosevelt's grave error was much worse. While accumulating all this power at the federal level, this, as he phrased it "instrument of unimagined power for the establishment of a morally better world" he seemed to forget one thing. Maybe it happens to all those who try to play god over others. They forget that they are mortal, and one day will die. When he was centralizing all that power unto himself, to accomplish all those good things that couldn't be done in a timely manner if we followed a "horse and buggy" Constitution, did he ever stop to think that he might be gathering all those powers for someone who would come after him and use them to hurt the people? Did he ever consider that he might be handing us over to some "military industrial complex" to do with us as they willed?

That is Franklin Roosevelt's gravest error, and where he most betrayed us. He didn't understand or agree with the founders about the dangers of despotism and demagoguery. Instead he heard the siren song of dictatorship, and imagined how much could be accomplished if the resources of the nation could be brought to bear in an efficient, modern way. He did consolidate the nation's strength, and did launch us into being the world's superpower. However, he did it by removing from us the consciousness of how to be self governing. Now, as all the debts come due, and the chickens come home to roost, the American people need to regain the kind of freedom we lost at the time of the New Deal. Otherwise, the sorrows of the collapse of our empire will bite us very hard indeed, and our descendants will be burdened with a formerly free, debtor nation incapable of self government.

Finally, and once again in FDR's defense, many of the excesses of big business that he was trying to fix were terrible, and needed fixing. Nonetheless, his mistake and the mistake of almost every one at the time, was thinking that only the federal government could control the runaway corporations. That mistaken idea was placed in our minds by that wrong headed decision of the U.S. Supreme Court when it was used to establish the concept of "corporate personhood" in 1886.

"Corporate personhood" ignited an engine that worked to systematically dismantle America's original plan of local community self government, usurping the powers of economic self government from states and localities. By the time Mr.

Roosevelt was finished, most of the powers and responsibilities of social self government (the social programs) had likewise been usurped from those same local and state governments, and invested in the federal government, worsening the effects of that original engine of destruction. In addition, FDR ignited a second destructive engine, in the form of Social Security and federal socialism in general, that has worked as an addictive, corrosive poison on the communities and families of America.

With both of those engines of destruction operating at full throttle, the stage was set for the inevitable third great blunder in the dismantling of the American republic, the usurpation by the federal government of the powers of local community moral self government. That is the subject of the next chapter.

Footnotes:

1. *FDR's Folly*, Jim Powell, (Crown Forum, NY, NY, 2003), p.217-218

2. Ibid, p.220

3. *Witness to a Century*, George Seldes, (Ballantine Books, New York, 1987) p.383

4. *Democracy by Thomas Jefferson*, Selected and arranged by Saul K. Padover, (Greenwood Press, Publishers, New York, NY 1969), Copyright 1939 by D. Appleton- Century- Company, p.46,47

5. Ibid, p.261

6. *Democracy in America*, Alexis de Tocqueville, J.P. Mayer- Ed., (Anchor Books Garden City, NY 1969), p. 62-63

7. *FDR's Folly*, p.210

8. Ibid, p.150

Chapter 3

How the First Amendment Was Turned Precisely on Its Head

"Congress shall make no law respecting an establishment of religion, or prohibiting the free exercise thereof; or abridging the freedom of speech, or of the press; or the right of the people peaceably to assemble, and to petition the Government for a redress of grievances."

First Amendment to the Constitution of the United States of America

As we continue an examination of the three major blunders resulting in the dismantling of America's experiment in self government, we will look at the error that was accomplished last; the complete twisting of the First Amendment. This stage of our examination should elevate our thinking in two ways. First of all, it will shock folks to realize how deeply we have all been hoodwinked on this issue. The backward, sideways, and convoluted process used in twisting the First Amendment is typical of how all three major blunders were accomplished. A closer look at the true use of the First Amendment (mostly in the next chapter) will bring the damage of all three major blunders into focus, helping to awaken a long dormant vision of how American liberty was intended to work.

The United States of America, in the first part of the Twenty First Century is a nation struggling with our most basic value, that of unity. The tragedy of this great national disunity is that it is largely driven by our misbegotten devotion to a flawed myth, namely that there must be a separation of church and state. This myth of separation of church and state is both impossible to achieve, and dangerous to pursue. In following this dark star, we have painted ourselves into a corner of national division, incoherent law, and an almost complete collapse of the consciousness of citizenship and self government. On the bright side, by considering how this change has come about and regaining a vision of the true use of the First Amendment, we might reverse the blunder and begin to re-acquire, for our people and our descendants, the great blessings of liberty.

Don't misunderstand. While a separation of church and state is impossible, it is possible to not have religious ceremonies conducted at government functions, to have no officially sanctioned religion. That is possible.

On the other hand, to insist that we will not have any morality taught, or any morality informing the passing of laws, or any morality guiding how we hand out public welfare, or any morality about what we think is right and wrong about education, or any other imaginable infringement of church into state. That is impossible.

There was a great social cliché from the 1960's that we can't legislate morality. At first glance, like a lot of the stuff out of the 60's, it sounds great. Folks like to do immoral things, and hearts and minds can't be changed by passing laws. But when looked at in a deeper way, it is revealed as pure drivel, because every law ever passed is an attempt to legislate morality, at least as it involves actions. Every law, from laws against murder and theft to laws about corporate policy or land zoning are based on someone's idea about what is right and wrong. Once enacted into legislation, these moral opinions are given the force of law, and imposed by the power of the state.

Take, for example, some of the most basic moral lessons we teach in this society. Who says that kindergartners have to line up in rows, and that girls should go to the girl's room, and boys go to the boy's room? What the hey, if we're going to have a total nihilism, why should they have to line up, or take turns, or be educated in the first place? And who says they shouldn't hit each other?

So okay, we'll teach some morality. The question then becomes, "whose" morality will be taught? The founders recognized this inevitable intertwining of morality, education, and religion before the Constitution was even written, in the Northwest Ordinance (1787), which states,

"Religion, morality, and knowledge, being necessary to good government and the happiness of mankind, schools and the means of education shall forever be encouraged."

As a short aside, this dedicated use of public education to instill morality was seen as necessary by the Founders, who lived in a mostly agrarian society where they spent a great deal of time with their children. Today, when parents spend much less time with their children, many argue that any morality should be taught at home, and the schools should be reserved for teaching the values of the state. This situation makes one wonder what kind of morals, or lack thereof, some want our children to have.

That dovetails with a much larger point. Thomas Jefferson, immediately after penning the Declaration of Independence, returned to the Virginia House of Burgesses and rose to advocate for doing away with the Church of England as the established church of Virginia. Jefferson said at that time,

"To compel a man to furnish contributions of money for the propagation of opinions which he disbelieves, is sinful and tyrannical."

Given the wide diversity of opinion in this nation on almost any subject touching law and morality, how are any opinions mandated from the level of the federal government without forcing someone to “furnish contributions of money for the propagation of opinions which he disbelieves…"? It is impossible not to violate someone’s beliefs if morality is to be legislated at the federal level. So the question becomes not only whose morality will be legislated and taught, but also what is the appropriate level of government to do this legislating?

This is the point the Founders came to in writing the First Amendment.

The first ten amendments to the Constitution, known as the Bill of Rights, came about because many of the original states approved the Constitution only on the condition that certain provisions would be added limiting the powers of the central government, and reserving certain rights and powers to the people and the states. The vast majority of the populace insisted on these provisions, because they wanted to prevent the kinds of religious and political oppression they had seen acted out by the strong central governments of Europe.

When the First Congress passed the First Amendment, and sent it to the states for ratification, it was never intended to be what it has become, a limit on what the states can legislate regarding speech, press, or religion. What's more, Congress did consider such limits on the states, and rejected the idea, or to be more precise, the ideas. One of the two proposals which were later combined into the First Amendment dealt with speech and press, and the other dealt with religion.

In the book, "Religious Liberty in America," Glenn T. Miller writes,

"The history of the wording of the first clause of the First Amendment is significant for its interpretation. The House of Representatives first adopted this reading: "Congress shall make no law establishing religion, or prohibiting the free exercise thereof, nor shall the rights of conscience be abridged." This was the most comprehensive form proposed. Two problems appeared in the Senate. The first problem was a movement to change the wording in the direction of permitting a multiple establishment of religion throughout the nation. One form that this proposal took was: "Congress shall make no law establishing any particular denomination of religion in preference to another or prohibiting the free exercise thereof, nor shall the rights of conscience be abridged." This was defeated. The second problem was a concern that the federal government not be permitted to interfere with religious establishments where they either existed or might exist. This concern shaped the wording decisively. The section on the rights of conscience was deleted and stress was placed on the prohibition of congressional action. The Senate sent this version to the House: "Congress shall make no law establishing articles of faith or a mode of worship, or prohibiting the free exercise of religion." Since this leaned too far in the direction of the New England type of Holy Commonwealth, the House finally passed this version: "Congress shall make no law respecting an establishment of religion, or prohibiting the free exercise thereof." The Senate concurred. In its final form, the First Amendment was designed to prevent any federal interference with religion. Congress could not pass a law establishing a church; nor could it pass a law disestablishing a church. The question of faith was, thus, reserved to the states for their action and their action alone. Should it prove necessary to pass laws regulating religion, as it would be if the churches were to hold property, they would be state laws." [1]

Make no mistake, this is very radical stuff. It means that the states were allowed to set up official religions, while the federal government wasn't. This is based on the word "respecting" included in the language of the First Amendment.

This might sound like utter blasphemy to people raised with the modern myth that there has to be a total wall of separation between church and state, but the fact of the matter is that many of the original states had established religions, and there was no thinking that this was in any way repugnant to the Constitution. In fact, taxes to support churches were levied well into the 1800's and requirements that office holders swear to religious beliefs were on the books until as late as the 1940's. It's true that they had been largely ignored since the 1850's, but they were on the books, and they fell into disuse only because of popular fashion, and not due to any constitutional problems.

We can find verification of this interpretation of the First Amendment by looking at the words of no less a friend of liberty than Thomas Jefferson (who first coined the phrase "wall of separation between church and state"). Consider "The Kentucky Resolutions," which he wrote (anonymously because he was John Adams' Vice-President at the time) in 1798, in opposition to the Adams' administration's Alien and Sedition Acts. In Section 3, he writes:

" Resolved That it is true as a general principle, and is also expressly declared by one of the amendments to the Constitution, that "the powers not delegated to the United States by the Constitution, nor prohibited by it to the States, are reserved to the States respectively, or to the people"; and that no power over the freedom of religion, freedom of speech, or freedom of the press being delegated to the United States by the Constitution , nor prohibited by it to the States, all lawful powers respecting the same did of right remain, and were reserved to the States or the people: that thus was manifested their determination to retain to themselves the right of judging how far the licentiousness of speech and of the press may be abridged without lessening their useful freedom, and how far those abuses which cannot be separated from their use should be tolerated, rather than the use be destroyed. And thus also they guarded against all abridgment by the United States of the freedom of religious opinions and exercises, and retained to themselves the right of protecting the same, as this State, by a law passed on the general demand of its citizens, had already protected them from all human restraint or interference. And that in addition to this general principle and express declaration, and the more special provision had been made by one of the amendments to the Constitution, which expressly declares, that "Congress shall make no law respecting an establishment of religion, or prohibiting the free exercise thereof, or abridging the freedom of speech or of the press": thereby guarding in the same sentence, and under the same words, the freedom of religion, of speech, and of the press: insomuch, that whatever violated either, throws down the sanctuary which covers the others, and that libels, falsehood, and defamation, equally with heresy and false religion, are withheld from the cognizance of federal tribunals. That, therefore, the act of Congress of the United States, passed on the 14th day of July, 1798, intituled "An Act in addition to the act intituled An Act for the punishment of certain crimes against the United States," which does abridge the freedom of the press, is not law, but is altogether void, and of no force." [2]

In short, Jefferson, and the framers of the Constitution understood the First Amendment to mean that it absolutely forbade the federal, or general, government from restricting any speech, censoring any book or paper, or establishing or interfering with any religion. On the other hand, they saw that it was perfectly proper for the states to be involved with any of those activities, if the citizens so decided in a free republic.

Just in case someone might think that the preceding thoughts from Thomas Jefferson came in the heat of battle with John Adams, and were later repented of, consider what President Jefferson said on the occasion of his second inauguration in 1805,

"In matters of religion, I have considered that its free exercise is placed by the Constitution independent of the powers of the general government. I have therefore undertaken, on no occasion, to prescribe the religious exercises suited to it; but have left them as the Constitution found them, under the direction and discipline of state or church authorities acknowledged by the several religious societies."

Within the context of state control, Jefferson fought vigorously for minimal government, which is why we can find so many of his writings calling for an almost absolute freedom of speech, press, and religion. Regardless, he would have clearly been against establishing even his own ideas of religion at the federal level.

That's the way things stood in this country, at least until the passage of the Fourteenth Amendment. In 1868, when the Fourteenth Amendment was ratified as part of reconstruction after the Civil War, uncertainty and confusion reigned in Washington D.C. No one knew how to put the country back together again, and the victorious North didn't want to lose in Congress what had been won on the battlefield. So one thing the "Radical" Republicans wanted to ensure was that state and local laws were enforced equally, especially in regard to the just freed slaves. For that purpose, they enacted the first section of the Fourteenth Amendment, which reads.

"All persons born or naturalized in the United States and subject to the jurisdiction thereof, are citizens of the United States and of the State wherein they reside. No State shall make or enforce any law which shall abridge the privileges or immunities of citizens of the United States, or shall any State deprive any person of life, liberty, or property, without due process of law; nor deny to any person within its jurisdiction the equal protection of the laws."

Some people think this all important first section of the Fourteenth Amendment is unnecessary, as the Constitution already guarantees equal enforcement of the laws, but they overlook the fact that whether or not freed African-Americans could be full citizens was the central question that had been denied in the infamous Dred Scott decision. Rep. John A. Bingham, of Ohio, the chief author of the amendment, was absolutely correct in bringing the whole notion of the first section of the Fourteenth forward because of Dred Scott and because we consequently needed a Constitutional delegation of power in order for Congress to have clearly legitimate authority in pursuing a civil rights agenda. Mr. Bingham once said, in advocating ratification of the Fourteenth, that, "It is a simple, strong, plain declaration that equal laws and equal and exact justice shall hereafter be secured within every state..."

So what does this have to do with the First Amendment? Unfortunately, all the separation of church and state stuff grew out of wrongly applying the First Amendment to the states, and that is based on a misuse of the Fourteenth Amendment. To once again resort to Mr. Miller's "Religious Liberty in America",

"These problems arose after the passage of the Fourteenth Amendment broadened the authority of the Federal Government. They would not have arisen under the original wording of the Constitution and the First Amendment, nor would many of the issues that divide us today have arisen under it. To cite one example, if the state of New Jersey had chosen to promote religious rather than public education, it would have been entirely within the Constitutional provisions to do so. It is not surprising, therefore, that few cases concerning religious matters reached the Supreme Court before the Civil War." [3]

The only correction to be made to Mr. Miller's thinking is to point out that these changes didn't occur immediately after ratification of the Fourteenth Amendment. Indeed, given the moral temper of the times, if the American people circa 1868 would have even suspected that approval of the Fourteenth would result in federal mandates of atheism in the schools and pornography in the stores, they would never have ratified it.

Even though the Fourteenth Amendment was intended to ensure the rights of full citizenship to African-Americans, it was only used for that purpose in a confused and halfhearted way, and a lot of that confusion has stayed with the issue until the present day. The primary use the Fourteenth Amendment was put to in the 1800's was to bestow most of the rights of American citizenship onto private interstate corporations, making them immune to most state controls, as was detailed in the first chapter of this manifesto.

To repeat a quote uttered by Justice Hugo Black in 1939 from that chapter,

"Of the cases in this court in which the Fourteenth Amendment was applied during its first fifty years after its adoption, less than one half of one percent invoked it in protection of the Negro race, and more than fifty percent asked that its benefits be extended to corporations." [4]

It only gradually started to be applied to both civil rights and First Amendment issues well into this century, after the 1930's. Actual enforcement of the Fourteenth Amendment, as written and intended; to ensure full citizenship for all, regardless of race, finally began in the 1960's as a result of the Civil Rights Movement.

So the question becomes, how did the First Amendment get dragged into this? It was sixty years after the ratification of the Fourteenth Amendment before the Supreme Court started applying speech, press, and religious standards onto the states, using the rationale that the First Amendment was to be applied to the states by the Fourteenth Amendment's "privileges or immunities" language; that the First was contained within the Fourteenth Amendment. The subject didn't even come up until 1905. Here's where it starts to get all sideways, backwards and convoluted, so be prepared. The beginning of the fallacy can be traced back to 1875 and the case of *U.S. v Cruikshank*, 92 U.S. 542,552.

Cruikshank was a case in which a group of African-Americans was seeking redress in the Supreme Court, under the Fourteenth Amendment. They had been repeatedly accosted by white citizens when they (the blacks) tried to attend peaceful political meetings. Since the Court was in no mood, in the waning days of Reconstruction, to see the Fourteenth Amendment properly applied, they ruled against the blacks, seeing nothing being done wrong by the State of Louisiana, and hence no trigger for the Fourteenth Amendment. In a snide little piece of dictum to the side, they let it be known that if said group had been meeting to petition the federal Congress, then the court might have ruled in their favor.

Key parts of the key paragraph read,

"...right of people...petitioning Congress. If it had been alleged in these counts that the object of the defendants was to prevent a meeting for such a purpose, the case would have been within the statute, and within the scope of the sovereignty of the United States."

There are three points in response.

First, the Court here makes the original mistake of misreading the First Amendment. Even if some group of citizens is meeting to petition the Federal Congress, the First remains solely a limit on congressional action. The Congress of the United States can't make a law to try to stop them, but the states remain free to. It does not, even then, become an individual right which the various states are required to protect. To offer an extreme argument, are the states required to allow even riotous behavior to continue if the participants claim to be meeting to petition the federal Congress?

The Court is here begging, in a small way, the same question it continues to dodge, in a big way, today. How can a limit on Congress magically become a guarantee of individual privilege, and hence a limit on the States instead?

Second point. A more sound legal approach and better advice for the Court to have given would be for the plaintiffs to attempt to demonstrate that the State of Louisiana was providing protection of the laws in an unequal manner. It would be easy enough to prove that the peace officers of Louisiana wouldn't allow their white citizens to be marauded in a like manner.

Third point. The race of the plaintiffs was mentioned a number of times in the Court's decision, undoubtedly so that future generations would realize what was really going on here. Those in the future would then hopefully forgive them for so nakedly grasping at any straw of rationale to avoid enforcing the already (by 1875) too radical Fourteenth Amendment. That also explains their little falsely friendly piece of advisory dictum; it was a racist joke for the ages. In the final analysis, this has to be one of the ugliest rulings in the history of the Supreme Court. Not only should they not have fiddled with the First Amendment in this way, but they should have recognized that the State of Louisiana was not enforcing the laws in an equal manner, and mandated federal intervention on the basis of using the Fourteenth Amendment in a legitimate way.

That's the sideways part. Now for how all this came in through the back door. In *Patterson v Colorado*, 205 U.S. 454, 462, (1905), the Court upheld a Colorado law prohibiting the publication of subversive literature. In his lone dissent, Mr. Justice Harlan held forth on the need for the entire First Amendment to be contained within the power of the Fourteenth Amendment. He forcefully argued that we need total freedom of speech and press in order to be an American society, and yet the only legal precedent cited for this view was that little piece of dictum from Cruikshank. Even that revered ruling he twisted out of all recognition, taking what was a limited aside, and converting it into a mandate that the entire First Amendment must be applied to the states, and that the country must consequently be thrust into absolute freedom of speech and press. His dissent is so powerful, (Probably the best single court statement ever written advocating our modern reading of the First Amendment), and later proved to be so influential, that it will be presented here in full.

"I cannot agree that this writ of error should be dismissed.

By the First Amendment of the Constitution of the United States, it is provided that 'Congress shall make no law respecting an establishment of religion, or abridging the freedom of speech, or of the press, or of the right of the people peaceably to assemble and to petition the Government for redress.' In the Civil Rights cases, 109 U.S.1,20, it was adjudged that the Thirteenth Amendment, although in form prohibitory, had a reflex character in that it established and decreed universal civil and political freedom throughout the United States. In United States v. Cruikshank, 92 U.S. 542, 552, we held that the right of the people peaceably to assemble and to petition the Government for a redress of grievances one of the rights recognized in and protected by the First Amendment against hostile legislation by Congress was an attribute of 'national citizenship.' So the First Amendment, although in form prohibitory, is to be regarded as having a reflex character and as affirmatively recognizing freedom of speech and freedom of the press as rights belonging to citizens of the United States; that is, those rights are to be deemed attributes of national citizenship or citizenship of the United States. No one, I take it, will hesitate to say that a judgment of a Federal court, prior to the adoption of the Fourteenth Amendment, impairing or abridging freedom of speech or of the press, would have been in violation of the rights of 'citizens of the United States' as guaranteed by the First Amendment, this, for the reason that the rights of free speech and a free press were, as already said, attributes of national citizenship before the Fourteenth Amendment was made a part of the Constitution.

Now, the Fourteenth Amendment declares, in express words, that 'no State shall make or enforce any law which shall abridge the privileges or immunities of citizens of the United States.' As the First Amendment guaranteed the rights of free speech and of a free press against hostile action by the United States, it would seem clear that when the Fourteenth Amendment prohibited the States from impairing or abridging the privileges of citizens of the United States it necessarily prohibited the States from impairing or abridging the constitutional rights of such citizens to free speech and a free press.

But the court announces that it leaves undecided the specific question whether there is to be found in the Fourteenth Amendment a prohibition as to the rights of free speech and a free press similar to that in the First. It yet proceeds to say that the main purpose of such constitutional provisions was to prevent all such 'previous restraints' upon publications as had been practiced by other governments, but not to prevent the subsequent punishment of such as may be deemed contrary to the public welfare. I cannot assent to that view, if it be meant that the legislature may impair or abridge the rights of a free press and of free speech whenever it thinks that the public welfare requires that to be done.

The public welfare cannot override constitutional privileges, and if the rights of free speech and of a free press are, in their essence, attributes of national citizenship, as I think they are, then neither Congress nor any State since the adoption of the Fourteenth Amendment can, by legislative enactments or by judicial action, impair or abridge them. In my judgment the action of the court below was in violation of the rights of free speech and a free press as guaranteed by the Constitution.

I go further and hold that the privileges of free speech and of a free press, belonging to every citizen of the United States, constitute essential parts of every man's liberty, and are protected against violation by that clause of the Fourteenth Amendment forbidding a State to deprive any person of his liberty without due process of law. It is, I think, impossible to conceive of liberty as secured by the Constitution against hostile action, whether by the Nation or by the States, which does not embrace the right to enjoy free speech and the right to have a free press."

And so Mr. Justice Harlan concluded, in 1905. A few points are in order, before moving ahead with the narrative of what happened to the First Amendment. In the second paragraph, he seems to be saying that free speech and press could not have been restricted by the Court because it was part of a national citizenship. This is a very technical but important mistake. The real reason the Court could make no such limit was Congress could make no law, and therefore the Executive has nothing to enforce, and the Court has nothing to adjudicate. Contrast Harlan's view with Thomas Jefferson's, quoted from "The Kentucky Resolutions" that issues of speech, press, and religion "... are withheld from the cognizance of federal tribunals."

Also in the third paragraph, his reliance on the Thirteenth Amendment is misconceived. The Thirteenth Amendment reads,

“Neither slavery nor involuntary servitude, except as a punishment for crime, whereof the party shall have been duly convicted, shall exist within the United States, or any place subject to their jurisdiction."

This amendment is clearly intended to apply to the states, having a "reflex character" as Harlan terms it, and is not, like the First Amendment, a limit only on Congress. The ruling he cites has nothing to do with the First Amendment, and he should be ashamed of equating the two amendments in this way.

In the third paragraph, he is again making the leap, as in Cruikshank, where a limit on Congress is changed into a right, which in turn becomes a limit on the states.

In the Fourth paragraph, where he can't assent to the idea that legislatures can limit speech or press based on concerns of public welfare, he disagrees with another of Mr. Jefferson's views, this also from "The Kentucky Resolutions" quoted earlier "...that thus was manifested their (the state's) determination to retain to themselves the right of judging how far the licentiousness of speech and of the press may be abridged..."

In the fifth paragraph, this "due process" stuff doesn't mean that states can't restrict liberty. Of course they can, when someone is convicted, by due process, of violating a law. It also doesn't mean (and it occurs in both the Fourteenth and Fifth Amendments) that the states are restricted from making certain types of laws limiting personal liberty. But it does mean that they must follow due process when enacting and enforcing them.

Finally, in the last paragraph, the good Mr. Justice Harlan might find it impossible to conceive of liberty without the absolute freedom of speech and press he calls for, but he had to ignore 130 years of prior American history to do so. What did he think he was doing, working up some fictitious society?

We will return to dispute the philosophical flaws of this famous dissent from the highly esteemed Mr. Justice John Marshall Harlan (he also, admirably, dissented from the infamous *Plessey v Ferguson* ruling, which established the onerous racist federal doctrine of "separate but equal") after following the history of the decline of the First Amendment to its finish.

Even though Harlan's was a lone dissent from the Court's opinion, it's noteworthy for a couple of reasons. First of all, in Patterson, the Court seemed to be engaging in a dialogue with Harlan, stating in its ruling that,

"We leave undecided the question whether there is to be found in the Fourteenth Amendment a prohibition similar to that in the First. But even if we were to assume that freedom of speech and freedom of the press were protected from abridgment on the part not only of the United States but also of the States, still we should be far from the conclusion that the plaintiff in error would have us reach."

The second reason Harlan's dissent is so important is that this is the only place the Court reveals any in depth thinking on this subject until 1947. What happened next is the Court said nothing on the subject for fifteen years, and then in the 1920's continued the dialogue by simply stating, without comment or explanation, that the Court saw the First Amendment contained within the Fourteenth Amendment.

In the first of these cases, *Gilbert v. Minnesota*, 254 U.S. 325, (1920), a case about a Minnesota law against advocating pacifism, Justice Brandeis, in dissent, saw no occasion to consider if the law violated the Fourteenth Amendment, but that such a subject was within the Court's domain was assumed. Then again, in *Gitlow v.New York*, 268 U.S. 652, (1925), the Court asserts, without stating why, that under the First Amendment, as contained in the Fourteenth Amendment, it has the authority to define the limits of speech and press. It then obscures and convolutes the point by agreeing with the lower court and upholding the conviction.

The court had previously ruled, during the First World War, that the phrase "no law" in the First Amendment didn't stop the Federal government from restricting seditious publications in war time. Combined with their assumed authority over peace time First Amendment issues, they then had the potential of generating some kind of federal definition of free speech, and applying it to the states. This all slid together when, under newly appointed Chief Justice Charles Evans Hughes, the Court overturned, for the first time (1931), some of the state's laws regarding press and speech. Stromberg v. California, 283 U.S. 359, and Near v. Minnesota, 283 U.S.

Minor cases of the same sort continued through the depression and the war years, until 1947, when the final great case in this chain of convoluted, backward mistakes around the First Amendment occurred. In *Everson v Board of Education*, 330 U.S. 1, the Court, using the now large number of minor cases as precedent, dictated at length about its power to define how intertwined a local school board could be with a local church. It was in this case that the terms "separation of church and state", "establishment clause" and "free exercise clause" entered the American judicial lexicon. And, in its typical convoluted, backward way, the Court upheld, for other reasons, the local school board's decision to use public buses to transport parochial school students.

These radical new concepts were left to simmer silently in the Constitution for more than a decade, and were then unleashed on a credulous and astonished nation. To again quote from Glenn T. Miller's "Religious Liberty in America",

"The most revolutionary action in the area of religion and education was in the cases of Engel v. Vitale (1962), School District of Abington Twp. v. Schempp (1963), and Murray v. Curlett (1963). The decisions in these cases outlawed the traditional practice of beginning the school day with devotions, usually prayer and Bible reading. The decisions were based on a strict reading of the First Amendment's anti-establishment clause, but they clearly went beyond the nation's traditional understanding of what that clause did or did not mean."

The public outcry against this new assertion of federal power was muted at the time, probably due to the fact that we were by then close to thirty years into a dependence on the federal government for the social aspects of government. Whereas previously social programs, such as public relief, indigent health care, old age support, and even education had all been generated locally, and were therefore dependent on the moral consciousness of the local population, by the 1960's everything had begun to fall under the sway of the federal government. Consequently, the move to place all issues of morality and moral education under federal control didn't seem to threaten the day-to-day well being of the citizenry, so they let this new ruling from the Court go unchallenged.

There then followed the entire odious train of rulings regarding freedom of expression, speech, and religion throughout the latter part of the Twentieth Century. Pornography had to be allowed in almost all communities, along with lewd and topless dancing, subversive literature, and flag burning. Then, in an arbitrary and inconsistent manner, the Court allowed some controls on speech, such as ethnic intimidation and hate speech laws.

At the same time, any expression of religious sentiment was banned from any public function, especially public schools. Thus our tortured national dance with the First Amendment has moved.

During this whole process the Supreme Court has projected a pretentious image of wisdom by first asserting that there can be no local, state, or federal controls on speech or press, and then relenting and admitting that the Court would define what limits there could be. This began in 1919, when Justice Holmes famously wrote in the case of *Schenk v United States,*

"The most stringent protection of free speech would not protect a man in falsely shouting fire in a theater and causing a panic." Further on he formulated this. "The question in every case is whether the words used are used in such circumstances and are of such a nature as to create a clear and present danger that they will bring about the substantive evils that Congress has a right to prevent."

These sound like wise words indeed, and would be very wise and entirely appropriate if uttered by a state legislator, or a county judge. But in the setting of a ruling by the U.S. Supreme Court, they must be seen for the beginning of a usurpation of power from state and local government that they are. Contrast this famous "clear and present danger" formulation with Jefferson's comments from, once again, "The Kentucky Resolutions"

"...that thus was manifested their (the state's) determination to retain to themselves the right of judging how far the licentiousness of speech and of the press may be abridged..."

So while the Court presents itself as being so liberal and wise, this whole process of prohibiting state and local controls, and then admitting that there did have to be some controls that the Court would deign to deliver to us, has really been just a disingenuous way of usurping some of the powers of self government from the states, the localities, and hence, the people.

In this whole process, from Harlan's dissent forward, there is an almost conspiratorial aura to the whole affair. This is not necessarily because there is an actual conspiracy abroad in the land, but rather because there is a school of philosophy abroad, which goes by the name of secularism, or secular humanism. This school of philosophy, or point of view if you will, tried to assert itself at the original writing of the First Amendment, with the idea that freedom of conscience should be protected from state interference. This same sentiment came up in Harlan's dissent, and now holds sway in this nation. The well meaning folks who advance it probably don't consider that they advocate violation of the Constitution. Rather, they wish so much that the Constitution did contain this concept of total separation of church and state, and total freedom of speech and press that they think it is there.

Whereas, the actual words of the First Amendment do not say that. Read it, presented at the beginning of this chapter. It is a single sentence that is clearly a prohibition on certain kinds of laws that the federal Congress is not to make. Since it is nothing but a prohibition on Congress, it is not a statement of privilege or immunity that accrues to the individual, and it is therefore not covered under the language of the Fourteenth Amendment. Consequently, just on the basis of a technical reading of the Constitution, the rulings of the Court are in error.

But of course, this is pretty small beer compared to the fact that the general population has bought into this myth, and has come to agree with the flawed philosophy behind it. This leads us to the philosophical discussion. The first issue to be wrestled with in this section is that separation of church and state is a myth impossible to attain.

Think about what a total separation of church and state would entail. If we were to thoroughly apply a literal reading of the establishment of religion clause (so that no law respecting any establishment of any religion or belief system could be passed) to all levels of government under the Constitution, including federal, the system becomes absurd. A total application of the principal that no law can be made respecting an establishment of religion, would leave the federal government unable to make any law or ruling, for or against, any entanglement between any level of government and any moral code. The same limit would apply to the states, counties, and localities. If there were some already existent laws based on someone's moral assumptions, they would have to be left in place, but any new moral realizations, such as the need for sound environmental policy, could not be established in law. No laws could be based at any level of government; on what anyone thought was right or wrong.

Given our modern propensity to thought crime excess, we might end up where it is illegal for an individual to have a moral, self governing thought, or to advocate anything. The individual is certainly the foundational level in self government, and no law means “no” law. What's more, the word "respecting" means respecting. No level of government could make any law, for or against, any religion or moral assumption. Only a numb nihilism (belief in nothing) would be allowed, and even that couldn't be enforced.

There are more good examples of how absurd this concept could become. You say no restrictions on press or speech? Then bring on the hard core child pornography and bestiality and let’s put them on billboards. No restriction on speech means get ready for riot, and for idiots who will yell "fire" in crowded theaters.

So separation of church and state, when we see that it necessarily means separation of the state from any unproven belief system, with the total freedom of speech and press that go with it, is definitely an absurd and impossible notion.

Pursuing this myth is so dangerous since it is impossible to achieve. Just as when the Court prohibited state and local controls on speech and press only to substitute their own controls, some have merely substituted their own, atheistically based belief system and installed that religion at the federal level. It is that school of philosophy known as secularism, or secular humanism.

Webster’s Unabridged Dictionary, 1979, definition of religion reads,

“3. (b) loosely, any system of beliefs, practices, ethical values, etc. resembling, suggestive of, or likened to such a system; as, humanism is his religion.”

Admittedly, this is not the only, or even the primary definition of religion offered by Webster (there are seven in this edition) but it is a valid one for our purpose, because it highlights the notion that separation of religion and state is impossible, and it points to why it is such a dangerous myth to pursue. What we have done in pursuing this myth is to install on ourselves an atheistically based secular humanist theocracy, which is very dangerous indeed.

The term “secular” or “atheistic theocracy” deserves a short aside. “Theocracy” means rule by God. Unless you are a devout believer who might point to ancient Israel, you must admit that no such thing has ever existed on Earth. What humans do get, such as in modern Iran, is a nation run by folks according to their ideas about God. So the word “Ideocracy” would be more accurate, and in a humorous way, more descriptive of what is going on in both Iran and America. All around the globe, we have “Ideocracy”, or government based around someone’s ideas about what is right and wrong, whether that includes God or not. Since “ideocracy” doesn’t carry the emotional weight, “theocracy” will be used here instead.

The point of the First Amendment was not to avoid having someone’s idea about right and wrong kept from the councils of government, but rather to prevent any particular belief system from being installed at the federal level. Since no system of government can avoid enshrining somebody's ideas, and since all laws are based on somebody’s ideas, the way the federal system is supposed to work is that when we, as a nation, come to some new moral conclusion, that idea, and no others, can be enshrined in the form of a new amendment to the constitution. This prevents establishing some particular belief system, but does allow us, as a nation, to grow and change.

The term "Atheistic Theocracy," while superficially a contradiction in terms, gets to the point about why it is so dangerous to pursue this myth of separation of church and state. We will never be able to arrive at that mythical, morally neutral foundation to our laws, but what has been done in trying to get there has been to systematically remove any reference to divinity in general, and the Judeo Christian God in particular.

The word atheism means, "Without God". It comes from the Latin, a -without, and Theo -God. By attempting to rid our entire civic structure of any reference to or reliance on God (or revealed ethics) we have succeeded not at building a wall of separation between government and any unproven, religious-like belief systems, but instead all we have done is to establish atheism (with-out-God-ism) as our official religion. No one is required to take an oath to it, but all laws that are based on any other belief system will be struck down as unconstitutional.

What’s more, Atheism, or Secular Humanism pretends to a moral superiority it hasn't earned: First, by keeping any reference to God out of its policies, using only what is thought of as reason, and second, by borrowing on the credibility that has been earned by the hard sciences. Secular Humanists then use this assumed moral superiority to simply dismiss any other point of view, and forge ahead with their social and political agenda, ignoring cries of religious oppression and cultural genocide.

The worst part is that they assert this supposed moral superiority while ignoring the fact that secular humanism has produced the most horror filled, immoral political regimes in history. Do the names Hitler, Stalin, and Mao ring a bell? Of course, the fact that they think their statistics and so called logic render them morally superior is simply proof of the point that every legal system will always have a set of unproven moral assumptions at its base, whether it's Secular Humanism with its statistics and so called logic, Catholicism with its traditions, Protestantism with its Bible, Islam with its Koran, or whatever.

The founders of this country wrote the First Amendment to prevent just the kind of oppression that occurred in Nazi Germany, and Communist Russia and China. Secular Humanism is just another religion among religions, (no worse, and certainly no better) and like all religions, it becomes especially dangerous only when it is given too much power in some centralized government. The founders clearly intended that no particular religion be established at the federal level, because they saw that a religion established at that level could exercise an oppressive advantage over all the other religions.

Seen in that light, the most important reason to get back to the original words, and reserve the powers mentioned in the First Amendment to the states and the people is because that's the only way to deconstruct the national theocracy we have become, the very thing the Founders worked to prevent. To sum up, this whole backward and convoluted process has set the First Amendment precisely on its head, taking the amendment the Founders intended to prevent the establishment of an official national belief system, and instead using it as a rationale to establish an official national belief system

Many will continue to argue that this is merely an attempt to revive the dead words of some dead white men. On the contrary, even though the words of the wise should be kept alive for their own sake, we should return to an honest use of the First Amendment because the society framed by the Constitution, one of local community moral self government, is far superior to our present system, and much more likely to produce unity, peace, and contentment in the citizenry.

First, we should get clear about the importance of using the First Amendment as it was intended. To do that, let us go back to the scandal of the usurpation of the First Amendment, and the dissent of Mr. Justice Harlan. In the final paragraph he wrote,

"I go further and hold that the privileges of free speech and of a free press, belonging to every citizen of the United States, constitute essential parts of every man's liberty, and are protected against violation by that clause of the Fourteenth Amendment forbidding a State to deprive any person of his liberty without due process of law. It is, I think, impossible to conceive of liberty as secured by the Constitution against hostile action, whether by the Nation or by the States, which does not embrace the right to enjoy free speech and the right to have a free press."

For the sake of deeper reasoning, let's set aside the previously discussed absurdity of actual enforcement of those rules, and admit that there must be some limits on speech and press: and even pretend it is appropriate for the federal courts to make those decisions. Even with all those stipulations, Harlan's definition of liberty is still flawed, because it posits a kind of atomized liberty. With his definition, each person as an atomized individual has exactly the same, homogenized liberties (and limitations) wherever in the nation they reside.

At first blush Harlan's atomized definition of liberty seems to empower the individual, and so must be moving in the best direction. He calls for everyone to have no limits on speech or press, so what could be freer than that? Remember though, that as soon as the Court removed all the powers to limit speech and press from the states and localities, it took those same powers to itself. The Court declared, in fairly specific detail, how far those freedoms should go, where they should be limited, and retained to the federal courts the power to make any further changes to the definitions of free speech and press.

So on deeper analysis it is seen that this atomized definition of liberty; this homogenized national sameness, actually dis-empowers and silences the individual because it renders almost any individual effort to change or improve the social environment pointless. Since all the real decisions in this atomized liberty are made behind closed doors thousands of miles away by authorities who don't have to care what the individual thinks, the individual citizen comes to feel that s/he has no real say in public affairs. Apathy is the inevitable result.

In addition to apathy, the atomized liberty of over centralized government also tends to cause division. For the few people who remain politically involved there is little or no reason to form together in mature compromise with geographical neighbors. Instead, since all the real decisions of moral and cultural government are being made at the federal level, it only makes sense to form together with whatever national party promises to place your kind of person in the Congress, the White House, and eventually the Supreme Court. Either our side forces our morality down their throats at the national level, or they will force their ideas down our throats. There is not very much reason left to form common cause with your neighbor on much of anything.

Consequently, to the normal, alienated, apathetic little person, with local community reduced to playing a never ending game of big brother may I with the feds, with its every move subject to federal nullification, said little person doesn't see much point in getting involved with the deliberations of local government. Nor does s/he sense any ability to make a difference in the deliberations at the federal level. Thus the sense of being involved with self government fades away from the little person, isolating them to family and a few friends, but not really connected to larger community. So the setting of the First Amendment precisely on its head results in an apathetic, alienated citizenry, dovetailing perfectly with the effects of corporate personhood and federal socialism.

Moreover, the usurpation of the powers of moral self government causes not only division, but deep hostility in the hearts of the American people for each other. Since, in this system, someone is always forced to "furnish contributions of money for the propagation of opinions which he disbelieves", we have been set at each other. Just as the quickest way to get two cats to fight each other is to tie their tails together, this perversion of our system has caused our mutual love of freedom to be used against us, causing us to engage in never-ending, vicious cultural warfare

The process of American decline started almost one hundred and fifty years ago. The next chapter will bring all these issues together, detailing the dynamics and associated issues of this decline, and offer an alternative vision of government, one that promises to restore to us the blessings of liberty.

Footnotes:

1. *Religious Liberty in America*, Glenn T. Miller,1976, (The Westminster Press, p. 75

2. *The Complete Jefferson*, Assembled and arranged by Saul K. Padover, Duell, (Sloan, and Pearce, Inc., NY, NY 1943), p. 128-134

3. *Religious Liberty in America*, p. 83

4. *Unequal Protection: The Rise of Corporate Dominance and the Theft of Human Rights*, Thom Hartmann, (Rodale, 2004). p. 157

Chapter 4

Downward Spirals and Upward Spirals

"...finally it reduces each nation to nothing more than a flock of timid and hardworking animals with the government as shepherd."

Alexis DeTocqueville 1835

Downward Spirals of Government

To sum up the three preceding chapters, and fill in some details, the dismantling of American free self government, in broad strokes, went like this. First, in 1886, the U.S. Supreme Court was abused to create the concept of corporate personhood, essentially letting the mechanism of corporate ownership off the leash of community control. This unleashing of the corporate beast ushered in the robber baron era, and the age of business monopolies was born.

Public alarm at the excesses of the robber barons brought about the progressive era and the rise of the Populist Party, approximately 1895-1905. This was the time of Teddy Roosevelt and trust busting. Mr. Roosevelt worked to roll back corporate power by using federal government regulations. Tragically, no one at the time seemed to realize that most of the excesses of corporations could be reversed by ending corporate personhood and placing the control of corporations back into the hands of the states and communities.

This also seems, in retrospect, the first era of the people generally beginning to doubt the competence and authority of local and state governments. The Food and Drug Act of 1905, direct election of senators, the Internal Revenue Service, the Federal Reserve, and other powers shifted from the people, states, and communities to the federal government between 1905 and 1920. This notion of centralizing government, based upon the sentiment that local and state governments had become somehow incompetent to solve modern problems, continued to grow throughout the nineteen teens and twenties (especially with the emergency powers granted to the federal government during World War I). At the end of the 1920's, the structure of federal economic regulation came apart, launching the Great Depression. The second great tragedy in this narrative is that rather than seeing the failure of centralized government to solve modern problems, the New Dealers decided to double down the bet, and greatly increased the power the federal government could exercise over the nation.

In Franklin Roosevelt's administration, instead of dealing with corporate abuse by revoking corporate personhood and restoring the control of corporations to our communities, the federal government unconstitutionally took over most of the powers of what can be termed social self government; the social programs that all societies must have in one form or another. Thus, during the 1930's, ongoing corporate personhood and the federal regulatory schemes that emerged as a response to corporate excess, accelerated the destruction of local community self government. By achieving so much of the New Deal agenda in constitutionally questionable ways, FDR greatly diminished the connection that the people had with the Constitution and constitutional process.

Worst of all, with the advent of socialism in general and Social Security in particular, Franklin Roosevelt loosed a second engine of destruction on America. Just as corporate personhood worked to erase the consciousness and reality of local self government from the people, Social Security (and socialism) operated like a corrosive, addictive poison to weaken the bonds of family and community that are so necessary in enabling the people to handle the reins of local self government.

The peripheral changes that either got worse or were initiated in the long term wake of FDR's usurpation of law making powers from the states in 1937 are too numerous to be detailed here. They include the Securities and Exchange Commission, FDA, EPA, The War on Drugs, Welfare, Department of Education, HUD, BATF, Department of Transportation, etc.

Adding to the corrosive socialism of the thirties and forties, in the 1960's Lyndon Johnson came along with what he called, "The Great Society" adding things like food stamps and Medicare to the list of public concerns controlled by the federal government. This amounted to a second metastasizing of the cancer of federal socialism. Suffice it to say that virtually the entire arena of what can be termed "social" self government has now been usurped or come to be unduly influenced by the federal government.

Since the social responsibilities of self government were no longer seen as the province of local communities, the necessity of raising a moral citizenry for a free republic to thrive no longer resonated strongly in our national debate. With the twin destructive engines of corporate personhood and federal socialism running at full throttle over the American landscape, a third issue that had been developing concurrent with the other two burst onto the scene. In 1947, the U.S. Supreme Court culminated that process by suddenly discovering, in *Everson v Board of Education*, that the Constitution forbids any kind of traditional moral influence on local, state or federal government. As has already been observed, since the Court upheld the right of that local school board to transport parochial school students on other grounds, this ruling went largely unchallenged at the time. Thirteen years later, when the Supreme Court used the doctrine it had planted then of "separation of church and state" to start throwing prayer out of public schools, followed quickly by federal mandates requiring local acceptance of pornography, lewdness, flag burning, insulting and seditious speech, and any other perversion of the First Amendment that could be concocted; the American people were emotionally and philosophically helpless to resist.

The Supreme Court had already come to be accepted as the only arbiter of a Constitution that was increasingly seen as an archaic and inscrutable document (mainly because the plain meaning of the words written there was rejected out of hand by the arbiters). Add to that the sentiment that these new changes didn't seem to threaten day–to-day national life, and the powers of moral self government were successfully usurped from the state and local governments by the federal government. This was the third great tragedy in this narrative.

Of course, there were any number of peripheral usurpations of the powers of moral self government that followed in the wake of *Everson v Board of Education*, and Murray, and etc. Foremost among these peripherals is *Roe v Wade*, which usurped from the states and localities the power of protecting the lives of the pre-born. This was done, as is typical of these usurpations, with no constitutional mandate, nor any amendment being enacted by the nation. Along the same lines, were the throwing out of anti-sodomy laws, laws against adultery in general and many other laws governing the moral lives of the populace.

With corporate greed off the leash of community control, and a runaway federal government having broken free from the chains of the Constitution, the complete overturning of the First Amendment, and the peripherals that followed in its wake, have worked like a capstone, sealing and protecting the overall fascist agenda. The usurpation of the powers of moral self government has worked in three major ways to keep that agenda going, and to work as a further engine destroying family, community, and national unity.

First of all it deeply divides the people. Since at least the cases that threw prayer out of public schools and even more so since *Roe v Wade* legalized abortion nationwide in 1973, the only way for a person to get the kind of moral government that he or she might like is to get the U.S. Supreme Court to be composed of like-minded members. That sets up a political dynamic that necessitates being in lock step with a national organization, and getting both the Congress and President that you desire. Any of us that care about lifestyle and moral issues (on either side of these issues) can feel very threatened and desperate to exert some control. The fact that any kind of local or state accommodation has been made impossible by the federal Courts drives us into the clutches of national organizations and creates the monolithic dichotomy of our modern politics. This monolithic dichotomy is a dynamic where each individual must become a supporter of one entire national agenda or the other to have even a hint of a chance to have our real concerns addressed. Then, we are not only at the mercy of the most distant and unaccountable level of government imaginable, but the people as a whole can't get together on the other major issues of economic and social self government. They are hopelessly pitted against each other around the issues of moral self government.

The second way that the overturning of the First Amendment hurts us is that the secular humanist priesthood it empowered has worked to inculcate the population with selfish and materialistic thinking. Schools and the media inundate us with the message that seeking our own self esteem is what life is about, and that sexual license, greed, and manipulation of others is okay.

If any state or locality tries to buck the trend, by casting doubt on the unproven theory that we came to be by a process of materialistic evolution, and that there might therefore be a moral component built into our lives, that is thrown out as an unconstitutional blending of church and state. Only the rankest form of materialism can be taught, because that is now the official belief. So when the young learn these lessons, and come to see themselves as material creatures having no higher meaning than satisfying their material appetites, we shouldn't wonder why. When these values leave us incapable of the kind of selfless, self-sacrificial thinking necessary for free self-governing communities to thrive, and so common in days gone by, we should be very concerned for our future.

The third way that the overturning of the First Amendment threatens us is closely related to the second. If someone had come to our nation in the 1920's and tried to impose an authoritarian government on us, we would have fought them with every fiber in our being. However, by removing the powers of moral self government from our communities, and spending decades inculcating us with selfish values, that same authoritarian government won't have to be imposed on us. Because of the breakdown in morality, and the resulting upswing in crime (we have more people in prison than any other nation in history) the people won't just accept an authoritarian government being imposed on them, they will demand it. Thus, the change in the use of the First Amendment has completely degraded our nation, while corporate greed continues to run away, and the federal government continues to gather more and more power unto itself.

Starting in the 1850's, it is hard to conceive of and come to grips with how wide a swath of destruction these changes have accomplished on the American republic. Nearly all the powers of self government, those of economic, social, and moral self determination, that were exercised at the state and local level in the 1850's, are now controlled at the federal, or even international level today. Local and state governments have become merely agents to carry out the wishes of the distant and unaccountable rulers. This is not the kind of free self government that the founders conceived, and it is no wonder that it is failing to deliver the blessings of liberty.

At this point we can begin to see the downward spiral that can be induced in human government. One bad policy, like corporate personhood, begets changes to the legal structure, thinking, and consciousness of the people, which lays the ground work for another bad decision; that of handing over the social responsibilities of government to the federal authorities. This in turn begets changes in the legal structure, the thinking and consciousness of the people, which also in turn, paves the way for another bad policy, the complete twisting of the First Amendment, and on and on the spiral descends.

In the first chapter, it was mentioned that everyone's ox will get gored in this book. That was an understatement. It is more like everyone has one or two sacred cows in this mess, and that in the end, your sacred cow won't just get gored, it will be slaughtered, bled out, skinned, butchered, and turned into jerky. This is quite a corner we have painted ourselves into, and to mix metaphors in a terrible fashion, each one of these sacred cows amounts to cords in our own Gordian Knot. Each time we try to loosen one of the cords it ends up tightening another part of the knot, rendering the whole mess unsolvable. If we are alarmed at the accumulation of governmental power at the federal level, we feel we must give more power to business. If we are concerned about big business, we give more power to big government. And if we are concerned about moral decline, we tend to give more power to the level of government that has driven that decline.

Leaving the peripherals to follow in the wake as we solve the three major blunders, the big three are things that most of us have come to see as essential parts of America. Corporations being free to maximize profit and wealth without answering to community standards; Social Security in particular, and federal socialism in general as the primary means of expressing compassion and social justice; and free speech, free press, and separation of church from any level of government, are three concepts that most will defend as absolutely vital to American life. Nonetheless, these three are the central pillars of a fascist agenda that is enslaving us.

Runaway corporate power is not the kind of economic liberty envisioned by the founders, nor does it generate the beneficial invisible hand of the marketplace identified by Adam Smith. Instead, our system has come to be dominated by a system of quasi governmental monopolies and approved collusion that would have appalled the founders. It stifles innovation and creativity, drives small entrepreneurs out of business, manipulates government to keep the labor force weak and compliant, and generally attenuates the benefits of the industrial revolution from reaching the masses.

Socialism and Social Security are not the only way to provide for the elderly and needy, nor are they the best way. Not only are these schemes inherently unstable financially, because they are pyramid schemes with expensive federal middlemen, more importantly, they erode our culture by dissolving the bonds of family and community, removing the vested interest that parents have in the character of their children. What is important to remember is that the elderly weren't starving to death on the streets of our nation before Social Security was enacted and they wouldn't do so if it were to end. Actually, since they used to live lives much more intertwined with family and community because it was the efficient way to do things, the elderly had lives with much more meaning and purpose than they do today.

Returning to the original use of the First Amendment might frighten some because we have been rendered fearful of freedom, coming to think that our friends and neighbors are just waiting for the day when we can enslave each other in some kind of religious theocracy. This is most foolish, and ultimately based on the fear that none of us should be free, because we, the people, can't handle those kinds of decisions. To the contrary, we should realize that the people could handle freedom as well as they did in the past, and that even if religious excess were to happen in some small towns, it would be self correcting as people could move, and change things if life got crazy.

On the other hand, by pursuing the unattainable myth of separation of church and state, we haven't arrived at some gloriously neutral government immune from the excesses of unproven belief systems. Rather, we have put ourselves under the thumb of an unelected secular priesthood that dictates right and wrong to the whole nation based on its own set of unproven beliefs. This is precisely the situation the First Amendment was enacted to prevent.

In enduring, accepting, and even clamoring for these changes, we have become profoundly alienated from our essential role in self government, and from each other. Consider the following prediction from Alexis DeTocqueville published in 1835.

"Thus, I think that the type of oppression threatening democracy will not be like anything there has been in the world before; our contemporaries would not be able to find any example of it in their memories. I, too, am having difficulty finding a word which will exactly convey the whole idea I have formed; the old words despotism and tyranny are not suitable. This is a new phenomenon which I must, therefore, attempt to define since I can find no name for it.

I wish to imagine under what new features despotism might appear in the world: I see an innumerable crowd of men, all alike and equal, turned in upon themselves in a restless search for those petty, vulgar pleasures with which they fill their souls. Each of them, living apart, is almost unaware of the destiny of all the rest. His children and personal friends are for him the whole of the human race; as for the remainder of his fellow citizens, he stands alongside them but does not see them;, he touches them without feeling them; he exists only in himself and for himself; if he still retains his family circle, at any rate he may be said to have lost his country.

Above these men stands an immense and protective power which alone is responsible for looking after their enjoyments and watching over their destiny. It is absolute, meticulous, ordered, provident, and kindly disposed. It would be like a fatherly authority, if, father like, its aim were to prepare men for manhood, but it seeks only to keep them in perpetual childhood; it prefers its citizens to enjoy themselves provided they have only enjoyment in mind. It works readily for their happiness but it wishes to be the only provider and judge of it. It provides their security, anticipates and guarantees their needs, supplies their pleasures, directs their principal concerns, manages their industry, regulates their estates, divides their inheritances. Why can it not remove from them entirely the bother of thinking and the troubles of life?

Thus, it reduces daily the value and frequency of the exercise of free choice; it restricts the activity of free will within a narrower range and gradually removes autonomy itself from each citizen. Equality has prepared men for all this, inclining them to tolerate all these things and often even to see them as a blessing.

Thus, the ruling power, having taken each citizen one by one into its powerful grasp and having molded him to its own liking, spreads it arms over the whole of society, covering the surface of social life with a network of petty, complicated, detailed, and uniform rules through which even the most original minds and the most energetic spirits cannot reach the light in order to rise above the crowd. It does not break men's wills but it does soften, bend, and control them; rarely does it force men to act but it constantly opposes what actions they perform; it does not destroy the start of anything but it stands in its way; it does not tyrannize but it inhibits, represses, drains, snuffs out, dulls so much effort that finally it reduces each nation to nothing more than a flock of timid and hardworking animals with the government as shepherd." [1]

The society De Tocqueville describes seems to be the one in which we find ourselves. The assertion here is that this woeful state is a direct and inevitable outgrowth of the three major usurpations, economic, social, and moral self determination that has resulted in an atomized definition of liberty being imposed upon us. This atomized, alienated, powerless mindset of the modern American must be contrasted with the involved, connected, and sincere citizen that used to be the norm in America, and would (it is here asserted) tend to be produced if these powers of self government were restored to the states and localities.

Upward Spirals

As we begin to consider the nature of the restoration of real power to local self government, it will be instructive to consider a modern platitude, namely that "freedom requires responsibility." While this bromide is undoubtedly true, the way it is used today, in the context of almost all the powers of self government being out of the reach of individuals, obscures the profound nature of the relationship between freedom and responsibility and has come to mean that we should blindly submit to and obey whatever those in power do with their "laws."

The much more important relationship between freedom and responsibility can only be seen when freedom is conceived as being mostly an attribute of local communities, and not of atomized individuals. When seen in this context, freedom will be self limiting and can thus be extended to each community in almost unlimited portion, because on those communities also falls the responsibility of meeting the challenges that nature throws in the way of all human societies.

An example will help explain this concept. Consider the case of a group of anarchists forming a community together, with the intention of having no governing rules. As a little time passes, the issues of how does the community acquire clean water comes up, along with the issues of how to dispose of sewage, and how to build and maintain roads. At first there might be a sentiment that the group will rely on voluntary action and community social pressure, but unless the local residents have risen to a consciousness far above what humans currently have achieved, that approach will fail, and the failure of the community to deal with the issues of healthy water, sewage and roads will destroy that community.

So okay, they will compromise and adopt some minimal local laws, not just around water, sewage and road issues, but things like power, indigent health care, public relief, corporate regulation, zoning and the like. At the same time, the local community will be empowered to deal with these challenges by having the power to determine what kind of public morality will be advanced, what will be taught in the schools, allowed in the local publications, and etc. Perhaps this hypothetical anarchist community will find ways to overcome the challenges without much resort to the heavy hand of government. But even if they do, the kind of liberty and cultural style they embrace will be naturally tempered by the responsibility of meeting the challenges which all human societies must overcome.

Here we can begin to see why the entire package of freedoms, powers and responsibilities usurped from the states and localities since the 1850's must be bundled together and returned to local community if the American system of local self government is to work again. On the other hand, if the powers and responsibilities continue to be separate, we can expect dysfunction to follow. If that local community can control what business does, and what is taught in the schools, but the responsibility for the social programs of medical care, public relief, environmental repair and the like stays in the hands of the federal government, we can expect the local community to be very licentious in its decisions. It will allow corporate and individual excess, because any resulting problems will have to be paid for by the feds. Severing the link between power and responsibility inevitably allows the making of irresponsible decisions.

If the social programs were the responsibility of locals, but the federal government controlled the education and corporate regulation, we could expect the values of big business to be taught the young, and the burdens of corporate excess to become overwhelming to local communities. Or, if the locals merely controlled business regulations, and the burdens of social responsibility and moral education fell to the feds, we could expect the local chamber of commerce to be very generous to corporations doing business there, since they would have none of the responsibility for fixing the ruined lives that might be left in the wake of runaway corporate greed.

We have already experienced what happens when the feds control corporations. The inevitable logic arises to give them all control.

Bundling enough of the powers and responsibilities of government together at the local level is critical if the true freedom of local self government is to be tempered by the responsibilities of the real world. Another example is in order. Say a community is very pro business, and encourages all kinds of industry. Their enthusiasm for commerce will be tempered if they are also required to pay for workers' compensation, disabled workers, and the ruination of the local environment. With those responsibilities to meet, the locals will see reason for some corporate regulation.

Or what of a community of socialists who want to regulate profit and capitalism out of existence. When they find that they can't establish a local economy, their enthusiasm for socialism will be tempered by reality. They might still have a strong ethic of social justice and environmental care, but it is safe to assume that they won't make any kind of profit and capitalism illegal.

LCMSG

Consequently, the first principle being proposed here is that the powers which have been usurped from state and local government since the 1850's be returned to where they were and as much as possible bundled together at the local level. This restoration of the powers of economic, social, and moral self determination, essentially a return to the kind of government defined by the Constitution, and intended by the founders, will henceforth be called Local Community Moral Self Government. This phrase is apt because every issue involved, from business and the environment, to social care and education, involves moral decisions. In the name of efficiency, this concept will be shortened to the acronym LCMSG most of the time.

Now it is time to consider what the United States of America would look like with LCMSG up and running, and the blessings of restored American liberty.

First of all, a nation with LCMSG would be far more diverse than today's nation. It would be a patchwork quilt of a nation with stark cultural differences between, at minimum, the states, and more likely (and wisely) between the towns and cities within a state, and even between neighborhoods in some cities.

Some places would probably have fewer limitations on press and speech than presently allowed by the feds, and some states would undoubtedly have more. Some would be very tolerant of sexual foibles, others would forbid them. Abortion would be forbidden in some localities, and legal in others. Some towns would have prayer in the schools, some wouldn't. Some places would teach evolution, while others would teach creation, and some would teach both. Some places would have full blown welfare systems while others might have old fashioned poor farms.

There would be immense cultural variations, and yet things wouldn't be all that different for most people. Many of the states would probably quickly institute some sort of secular humanism. That would be fine because under the Constitution, states are where such decisions should be made and where belief systems should properly be established. There would be regional differences. Maybe the southeastern states would tend toward returning to a Christian oriented moral education. The Midwest, California, and New York might be more secular humanist in nature. Imagine Utah being Mormon, while on the other hand, Colorado and Alaska are open to counties and localities establishing local official belief systems. Then we would have the kind of cultural variation within which everyone, no matter how strange or normal, could find a niche to thrive.

So what are the advantages to you, the individual? First of all, you would be free to live where you want. You could choose a state, town, or locality where the people thought as you think. There would be a universe of local culture styles from which to choose. You, the individual, could be part of a community with laws that are very agreeable to you. That kind of wide variety of cultural styles from which any individual might choose has to be one of the most meaningful aspects of liberty.

Moreover, once you moved there, you would have a great deal of power, as an individual under the federal and state constitutions, to persuade your neighbors to change things to be even more to your liking. This personal political empowerment is another very meaningful aspect of the traditional American definition of liberty.

Eventually, most moral issues will be settled in our local community, so we won't be constantly arguing over them with our neighbors. Sure, we might sit and make fun of the folks in the next community, and the problems they have because they don't do things our way, but we won't worry about them too much, because they won't have much say over how we run our community. Living lives of contentment and harmony within our local community would be one of the great blessings of liberty.

You see, most of these cultural/moral issues won't go away. Abortion and infanticide were controversial a thousand years ago, and they will most likely be controversial a thousand years from now. The same is true of homosexuality, welfare, medical care, the morality of education, and many other issues. The best we can do is enabling individuals to form into communities of agreement, where the issues they care most about are settled, because they and their neighbors agree on them. Then we can each live in the kind of environment we believe is best, and raise our children. We could minimize the problem identified by Jefferson, that "To compel a man to furnish contributions of money for the propagation of opinions which he disbelieves, is sinful and tyrannical."

Because we'd agree on so many basic issues, there would be a lot less arguing. We would have more time and energy to solve our other problems. The odds are, we as individuals would live happier, less stress-filled lives. In short, the felicity and harmony of the American people would increase if we were free and more empowered to control our own lives and communities. --- another great blessing of liberty.

In this kind of political regime we could expect the sense of community to once again assert itself in this country. Consider again the following insight from DeTocqueville, quoted earlier;

"It is important to appreciate that, in general, men's affections are drawn only in directions where power exists. Patriotism does not long prevail in a conquered country. The New Englander is attached to his township not so much because he was born there as because he sees the township as a free, strong corporation of which he is part and which is worth the trouble of trying to direct.

It often happens in Europe that governments themselves regret the absence of municipal spirit, for everyone agrees that municipal spirit is an important element in order and tranquility, but they do not know how to produce it. In making municipalities strong and independent, they fear sharing their social power and exposing the state to risks of anarchy. However, if you take power and independence from a municipality, you may have docile subjects but you will not have citizens." [2]

That would be another advantage to a more localized, community-centered political structure. It only stands to reason that re-empowering the communities would help to bring about a stronger sense of community. That stronger sense of community would in turn empower us to solve many problems without resorting to the heavy hand of government. That could be the greatest of the blessings of liberty and will be looked at more closely in a bit.

LCMSG and Corporations

Think about how much regulation of corporations is based on morality, and why it would be much better placed in local, rather than federal hands. When the regulation of business is under the control of federal authorities (or, unbeknownst to most of us, under the control of anonymous WTO boards, meeting in secret, issuing rulings that can't be appealed to any court or legislature) we come to these issues as a divided people, as consumers, versus workers, versus owners. The decisions handed down are the fruit of this divided dynamic, and if corporations are consequently legally empowered to be abusive, as with credit cards, lending practices, environmental damage, pension and bankruptcy abuses, and all the rest, then we, the people, just have to suck it up, and hope to win the next battle. Even if we do get a law passed that favors the little people, it might not be enforced, or might be repealed in the dark of night; or any of a number of stratagems the powerful can employ to thwart the will of the people. What's more, the preceding litany doesn't even mention outright corruption, where bribes and influence can be used by the wealthy to keep the workers and consumers in place.

At best, when the present system works as it was intended, federal controls amount to a letter of the law kind of control. If a corporation can meet certain legal guidelines (often written in cooperation with corporate officials) it is free to be as greedy and abusive as it can get away with. This aspect must be contrasted with the dynamic that would, and did, prevail when corporations weren't considered persons.

To understand this point, it is necessary to refer to the biblical concepts of the letter of the law versus the spirit. In the

Old Testament, there are given ten basic laws, and numerous minor laws which are to be fulfilled if God is to be pleased. In the New Testament, there is one law, love, and specifically love your neighbor as yourself. While it seems at first glance that this second law is much easier to live out, in actual life, the opposite is true. With the letter of the law, once the legalistic standard is met, then people are free to be abusive and oppressive. The law of love, while much less specific, calls us to give everything of ourselves, in every situation, and never leaves us free to become abusive or oppressive.

In the same way, when we sit down under LCMSG, at the community table to discuss giving a corporate charter to some enterprise, we come not as workers divided against consumers divided against owners, but as equal citizens of a community. Rather than asking if said enterprise can meet some list of federal guidelines, we can ask the simple question of "How does this business benefit the community?" That might seem like it would be easier than meeting federal guidelines, but in the end it would be a much more thorough and healthy control on the business, one which would involve the owners in self policing.

The question of benefiting the community goes to all the issues of business Once a business or two has been de-chartered because the people rose up against it after they didn't see it as benefiting their community, and there was no federal court ruling to protect corporations, other business owners would learn to concentrate on actually providing a benefit to the community. This would involve more than just clever public relations work, and would go to issues like low pay, taking too much profit out of the community, harming the local environment, leaving too many sick and injured workers to be cared for on the public dole, causing too many people to be in great debt, and all the other issues that might involve any business enterprise. All of these issues have to do in some way with moral/ethical reasoning, and hence fall under the "Moral" part of LCMSG.

It is entirely fitting that the government, at any level but especially the community level, should exercise these kinds of control over corporations. When a government charters any corporation it creates a kind of beast. Therefore it has an absolute duty to give the people a way to control that beast. When corporations are chartered at the local and state level, and can be de-chartered by the local lawmakers, then the beast is on the appropriate, short leash, and the beneficial aspects of incorporation can be entered into without the risk of corporations being able to rule over us. That is exactly the way it was before *Santa Clara County v Southern Pacific Railroad* in 1886. Shortly thereafter, at the start of the present era of runaway corporate greed, the so called Gilded Age, the people were scandalized that the owners and fat cats could be taking home twenty or more times the money than the average worker. That kind of greed wasn't heard of up to that time, and yet today it is seen as moderate profit compared to the average CEO making 400 times as much as the average worker.

To emphasize the point that runaway corporate greed wasn't the case in early America, consider again another quote from "Democracy in America" by Alexis DeTocqueville, "For all this conventional enthusiasm and obsequious formality toward the dominant power, it is easy to see that the rich have a great distaste for their country's democratic institutions. The people are a power whom they fear and scorn. If some day the bad government of democracy were to lead to political crisis or if ever monarchy appeared as a practical possibility in the United States, one would see the truth of what I'm saying." [3]

So the wealthy were not really all that happy with the rise of a democratic nation, and with the Civil War, and corporate personhood that followed in its wake, they took the opportunity to change things. What we have ended up with is a morality which says greed is good, and that there is no such thing as excess profit. The only alternative we are offered is an equally elitist socialism, which, while supposedly controlling the greed of business with a never ending list of regulations, would put us all under a totalitarian thumb, and (if experience can be guide) leave the rich and powerful in place to rule over us in a fascist oligarchy.

With LCMSG in force, we would have the tools to identify why greed is so bad, and to deal with it in a healthy, non totalitarian way. When we come to the table as a community, we see greed not as some good engine of progress (reasonable profit is that, but not excessive profit) nor as an inevitable force of class warfare that must be stopped by ending free enterprise, but rather as the cancer it is. Cancer in a living body is when one cell begins to grow, multiply, and take resources far in excess of what it needs or is appropriate, to the detriment of the larger body. When we have the kind of community consciousness that is engendered when communities have real powers of self government, we will just naturally feel repugnance toward the cancer of greed, and feel no duty or compulsion to accommodate it. Those who would incorporate, or conduct a business, would be members of the community, and would share those values, and those who didn't, would come to know that their greed was seen as a moral failing, wasn't welcome, and would behave accordingly.

One more advantage to having local and state control of corporations is that the people become much more aware of what it takes to make society, and an economy work. Consider another quote from DeTocqueville, "...in the restricted sphere within his scope, he learns to rule society; he gets to know those formalities without which freedom can advance only through revolutions, and becoming imbued with their spirit, develops a taste for order, understands the harmony of powers; and in the end accumulates clear, practical ideas about the nature of his duties and the extent of his rights." [4]

In 1939 there was a famous debate between Wendell Willkie and FDR's spokesman Robert Jackson, which elevated Willkie's stature enough to gain him the Republican nomination for President in 1940. During the debate, "Jackson also made a stab at explaining why there was conflict between government and business; 'The man who is in government is brought in contact with the problems of all kinds and conditions of men. Everybody's business is his business.' The private businessman, by contrast, 'has been intensely preoccupied with a very narrow sector of the world.'" [5]

This is specifically where the concept of corporate personhood comes in, and it is such a tragedy that it wasn't noticed at the time of FDR. Yes, that discussion that takes the interests of the entirety of society into consideration should take place, and did and would, at the state and local level, if there were no corporate personhood. If business could be de-chartered for not benefiting the community, with no federal courts preventing the states and localities from operating in that mode, then even the thinking of businessmen would start to become more holistic. Also, the thinking of all citizens would come into play, being heard in the counsels of government, with citizens becoming aware of the needs of business, and balancing that with the legitimate call for economic justice on the part of workers and consumers.

In other words, when we come together to this holistic discussion of how we can work together to meet the challenges that nature and reality throw at us, and how we can best incorporate whatever new technology that comes along, the kind of class war thinking FDR advanced doesn't even emerge. In fact, the lack of a class warfare ethic in this country, so lamented by leftist radicals of the European mode, is probably a residual throwback to the time before corporate personhood. The people as a whole understand and sympathize with the need for business to make a profit. The distinction between legitimate profit of a beneficial business and the excessive profit of greed is one that can't easily be made by the blunt instruments of federal corporate regulation. It is a distinction which comes easily to the fore if regulation of corporations is in the hands of local or state government.

During that same debate, one listener asked whether the threat of the concentration of government wasn't stronger than the threat of concentrated business. Jackson, defensive, said that the United States would never have concentrated government in Washington if business had not become so powerful. The states alone were obviously not sufficient to regulate big utilities, Jackson argued; 'How can a single state regulate Mr. Willkie?'" [6]

How indeed? It is certain that Americans need some way to regulate corporations, but it's a good bet that we would have had to wait for a long time for Mr. Willkie to respond that we should return the chartering of corporations to the states. Here, in this one instant in time, we can see the negative symbiosis, the unspoken collusion, between the forces of big business and big government.

LCMSG and Morality

Moving on past the issues of business, there is one more major aspect of LCMSG that would benefit society compared to today's way of doing things. That involves what can be called personal morality, and moral failings. One of the fundamental problems with centralized socialism is that it is very inefficient and unaccountable in comparison to local control. Some of the advantages inherent in local control can be seen by taking a close look at welfare.

Imagine welfare as a pool of fresh water. Everyone who needs some water can get some, and every productive citizen is required to contribute some water to keep the pool full. When the pool is maintained on the federal level, there is so much water it looks like an ocean. On that level, it doesn't seem to matter how many people are on or off welfare. The amount people can take out seems to have no limit, and the amount that individuals must contribute seems to remain the same, regardless of the number of people on the dole. In that context the producing citizen doesn't have a lot of interest in reducing the welfare roles, and is looked upon as mean spirited and selfish if he or she complains about the folks on welfare.

When this is put in the context of local control of public relief (as welfare used to be called), a different picture emerges. The pool of water no longer looks like an ocean, but is now like a lake, or even a pond. If more and more people are taking out water, the producing citizens have to contribute more to keep the pool full. When this starts to become burdensome, the local citizens will do what they can to reduce the relief roles. Tactics might include ostracism, shaming, and poor farms. More often, local citizens will cooperate to create jobs for the less fortunate. The thinking on the part of producing citizens is, "If we have to support them anyway, they may as well be producing something for the community." And voila! Instead of a welfare recipient, the community now has a productive citizen. Also, in the holistic reasoning engendered by LCMSG, the conclusions regarding dealing with public relief might well become decisive factors when chartering corporations.

Local communities would also be in a position to apply moral standards to recipients, which could greatly motivate recipients to become productive members of the community. The federal government isn't in a position to do that, because they are so distant, and have to rely on legal formulations, with no openly moral guidelines allowed to avoid the intertwining of church and state. If the recipient meets the letter of the law, they qualify. There is no place in the federal bureaucracy, for personal judgment, moral guidance, and simple human to human interaction. And yet, those very qualities which can be brought to bear on a local level, are the keys to preventing welfare from becoming a system of chronic dependence.

To be clear, this is now speaking directly to issues involving personal morality. This may involve local government being able to enact laws against vagrancy, fornication, adultery, sodomy, etc. If a local community sees certain actions as detrimental to the community, it could make laws against them.

It is important to add some thoughts to allay the fears of the secular humanist, free thinking crowd. When advocating the uplift of morality, it isn't intended to mean only traditional deistic morality, even though that mode of moral thinking is included.

This is an opportunity to fill in some of the vision of what a nation of morally self governing local communities would look like, and how utterly diverse and purposefully responsible it would be.

Take, for an instructive example, what a future city of San Francisco might look like with LCMSG in place. Assume that they continue to embrace legal and open homosexuality. Even then, with what some consider immorality institutionalized, there would still be a local morality, but it would have to pay its own way. If someone is incapacitated by sexually transmitted disease, that person would have to be supported by local taxes, and wouldn't be a source of federally based income, as is the case today. In order to prevent major problems with disease, there would be a well thought out set of local mores involving bath houses and singles bars. The local citizens, who had been involved in writing these laws, and establishing these customs, will try to make the local system work. That is all that is intended by this "trying to morally uplift the local community" stuff. It merely means that in a situation of Local Community Moral Self Government, the normal citizen will endeavor to make the local system work well. Even if the various local communities have widely differing and conflicting definitions of what is right and wrong (and they undoubtedly would), the denizens of those local communities would still tend to be moral by their own lights.

.On the other side of the ledger, to allay the fears of those who think this would result in a society of runaway debauchery; consider that the limits of earthly reality would be one of the major checks and balances in a truly free society. If San Francisco wants to continue embracing homosexuality, fine. However, that city would have to pay, out of the local purse, for the health care of all the patients its tolerance produces. While having to deal with its own problems wouldn't force the city to become homophobic, or force any other locality into any other form of intolerance, it would temper the local culture. It can easily be seen that if the education and laws in some community encourages total self indulgence and irresponsibility, that community would likely be bankrupt in short order. It might be hoped that the liberal cities would maintain their tolerant stance, but it is almost certain that they would modify some of their policies to keep from going broke.

This new architecture of government, combining as many of the powers of moral, economic and social self government at the local level of government as we wisely can, would first of all, be a move back toward the government designed by the founders. All three of the major usurpations of power by the federal government were brought about by wrongheaded actions (or inaction) by the Supreme Court, and can, therefore, be corrected by just a few instances of the Court's reversing itself, or being reversed by Congress.

The technical solutions to the dilemma will be addressed in future chapters. Of far greater import, is that in bundling this critical mass of the powers of self government at the local level, we create a social environment that tends to produce an involved, sincere, and well-meaning citizen. Once again, this is the greatest and most important blessing of liberty.

The only way to raise community consciousness is for the community to be truly empowered politically. It is only when the local populace has to balance the desire for a prosperous economy with the desire for a healthy community and environment that it will make good decisions about which corporations to charter. Only when that same local populace has to balance the desire for individual liberty in lifestyle choice with the need to provide health care and public relief to those who live those lifestyles will it come to wise decisions about what to allow. And only when the local populace has those responsibilities and powers will it be in a position to make wise decisions about the kind of moral education to impart to the young.

Finally, it is only when individuals are living in such morally self governing communities, wherein as individuals, they feel they can have a real influence on the decisions of local government, will that process begin to cause the individual to become a more moral and civic- minded person. Only when all three major aspects of LCMSG are combined will that positive dynamic, one that generates good citizens, begin to take hold.

When the local community must take total responsibility for social problems such as public relief, indigent health care, sewage, roads, power, water, and jobs, and at the same time decide what is taught in the schools about morality, what limits to put on any public exposure to pornography, lewdness, sexual behavior, drug laws, regulating corporate behavior, fighting words, intimidation, sedition, or any of the whole host of moral issues involving government, a healthy balance is struck. Then the individual citizen involved with making these decisions, and in solving the problems with which all societies are faced begins to see the benefits of a virtuous life, and contrarily, the harm that is done to society by an immoral, irresponsible lifestyle.

Things like fatherless or parentless children, the spreading of disease, substance dependency, obesity, violence, greed, and many other issues will always come at a cost to society, both morally and economically. By putting the responsibility, and hence cost, for these social problems at the local level, the individual is compelled to wrestle with them. Any honest wrestling in these areas will generally result in the conclusion that a society that goes too far in the direction of self indulgence and vice will end up morally and economically bankrupt. When these issues are solved at the federal level, the individual pays for them, but doesn't realize it because the pool of national resources is so large, like an ocean. Putting them at the local level reduces them to a pond, and puts the cost of these problems right in the face, and pocketbook, of the average citizen.

The average citizen, trying to make the system work, will tend to favor the kind of moral education and social environment that prevents the costly problems of social debauchery from arising in the first place. In sincerely attempting to uplift the morals of the citizenry, most honest people, and most of us are, will tend to see the importance of living a moral and responsible personal life.

Most of the Founders are in recorded agreement that only a moral people will be able to maintain a free society. As mentioned in the introduction, this simple truth only stands to reason because, as a nation loses the voluntary restraint of a strong personal morality, that same society, out of fear of itself, will call for stronger and more authoritarian government. Only a moral people will remain free.

The assertion here is that the reverse of that axiom is also true. Just as only a moral people will remain free, only a truly free and self governing people will see the reason to be moral. This is the greatest blessing of liberty; that it tends to produce involved, sincere, and intentionally moral citizens. With that aroused citizenry, the government, and especially the local branch of it, could be made to work very well.

Not only will LCMSG tend to produce that moral individual, but the even bolder assertion made here is that LCMSG (Local Community Moral Self Government) is the ONLY architecture of government that will produce that aroused citizenry. So yes, this is saying that it is imperative for us to get back to the Constitution and reinstate Local Community Moral Self Government, if we are to regain self government and the blessings of liberty. This is not to slavishly submit to the words of some dead white men, nor is it even that the government they left us is superior to the one we have today. No, the overriding reason to revive Local Community Moral Self Government is that no other form of government will tend to produce that good, involved, and morally-minded citizen necessary to make free self government work. What's more, any system of government that doesn't generate that kind of good citizen will inevitably decline into authoritarian, despotic rule.

In the book, "The Outline of Sanity", G.K. Chesterton advocated for what he called a peasantry, a populace which owns its own small plot of land, and therefore has a good deal of the reality of Local Community Moral Self Government. "Three acres and a cow" was his battle cry. He likened it to a brick, floating in mid air, among a rainbow of bricks. [7]

Such a thing seems impossible, until you are informed that he is referring to a Roman arch, and then it makes perfect sense. While a partially constructed Roman arch, formed of stone or brick mortared together in a round shape, is an object of derision because it makes no sense and looks like it will fall down, when it is completed, it is one of the strongest of all structures, because it uses a force of nature, gravity, which normally weakens structures, to gain more strength. Many of the arches built by the Romans 2000 years ago still stand.

In the same way, LCMSG seems to make no sense because it doesn't seem to be possible. But when we realize that such arrangements have been accomplished in the past, and that some still stand because they use the forces of nature to strengthen themselves where other structures get weaker over time, we see that all we need is a vision, some courage, and some perseverance to get it done.

Back again to Alexis DeTocqueville writing in "Democracy in America", "Only peoples having few provincial institutions or none deny the usefulness of them; that is to say, it is only those who know nothing of them who slander them." [8]

Just so; and we have a media/cultural elite that miss few chances to demean and ridicule local government and small community life.

On June 5, 1824 Thomas Jefferson, close to the end of his life, wrote the following in a letter to Major John Cartwright,

"My own State has gone on so far with its premiere ebauche; but it is now proposing to call a convention for amendment. Among other improvements, I hope they will adopt the subdivision of our counties into wards. The former may be estimated at an average of twenty-four miles square; the latter should be about six miles square each, and would answer to the hundreds of your Saxon Alfred. In each of these might be, 1st. An elementary school; 2d. A company of militia, with its officers; 3d. A justice of the peace and constable; 4th. Each ward should take care of their own poor; 5th. Their own roads; 6th. Their own police; 7th. Elect within themselves one or more jurors to attend the courts of justice; and 8th. Give in at their folk house, their votes for all functionaries reserved to their election. Each ward would thus be a small republic within itself, and every man in the State would thus become an acting member of the common government, transacting in person a great portion of its rights and duties, subordinate indeed, and yet important, and entirely within his competence. The wit of man cannot devise a more solid basis for a free, durable, and well-administered republic." [9]

So, we can see that the architecture of government proposed here is not without its historical advocates, and that some great thinkers have seen no better form of government possible this side of heaven. The potential benefits are multi fold, beginning with the idea that such a society would be more "durable" or stable.

The great benefit of LCMSG is, of course, the effect it would have on the individual citizen, and by extension, the citizenry as a whole. By setting up a form of local self government that is local enough that the individual has a real chance to affect real changes, and by allowing wide variations in local cultural styles from which the individual citizens are free to choose, the average citizen would feel much more attached to the workings of the law, and would tend to be a more involved, active, and moral person. Once again, this uplift in morality would not be limited to traditional, religious or Christian based morals, but would instead mean that the average citizen would sincerely be trying to make the local system of government work effectively. This benefit would be of inestimable value, and would prevent many problems from becoming problems in the first place.

What's more, this would be a much more scientifically based society, in that each state, county and village, could serve as a social laboratory, where different methods and solutions could be tried and compared with the methods of other communities for effectiveness. This has to be contrasted with the rather stilted (and unscientific) current method of letting the national elites thrash out the issue in the context of politically motivated, usually phony, rhetoric, and then impose a one size fits all "solution" that by definition can't be compared to the results of other methods because no other methods are allowed.

Constitutional Limits to LCMSG

Since this would be built around allowing wide cultural variations between communities which would greatly increase the options to the individual, the question becomes "What would be the limits to these local powers"? What would prevent them from becoming abusive and oppressive?" The answer is reality and the Constitution as written. As already explained, reality would have a way of bursting the bubbles of the most extreme utopians if the powers and responsibilities of government were bundled together at the local level

The other major control on runaway local extremism would be the U.S. Constitution as it is actually written. First and foremost among these would be the Fourteenth Amendment, which mandates that "No state shall...deny to any person within its jurisdiction the equal protection of the laws." No matter what laws a locality or state might enact, it is the federal government's job to ensure that all laws are enforced equally. That principle alone would prevent a great deal of mischief. Many local extremists and power mongers would be rendered more moderate by the certainty that whatever schemes they engaged in would apply to themselves equally with the least citizen in the area.

In addition to the Fourteenth Amendment, there are a number of other constitutional restrictions that would both limit local extremism, and empower individual citizens. Article IV, Section 4 requires that every state be a republic, so no one could set up little dictatorships or monarchies. Amendment 26 established the voting age at 18. Amendment 24 forbids poll taxes for any election of federal office. Amendment 19 ensures that women have the vote. Amendment 15 forbids the denial of rights based upon race. Amendment 13 forbids slavery. Amendment 8 forbids cruel and unusual punishments (and could be very important as local governments come under the sway of various belief systems). Amendment 7 ensures a trial by jury in civil actions. Amendment 6 ensures a speedy and public trial, with the defendant having right to counsel. Amendment 5 ensures that property can't be seized without due process.

Amendment 2 guarantees that individuals can keep and bear arms. In all of these amendments, and in other places in the Constitution, are found rights and protections for the individual against any governmental excess, but especially against the excesses that might come from local governments. These are some of the ultimate checks and balances that would work to keep a return to Local Community Moral Self Government healthy.

The constitutional protection that we will focus on for a moment is the Fourth Amendment, because it, like the Fourteenth Amendment, would play such a large role in the lives of individuals living in a system of LCMSG. Think of the situation of someone who likes to do something that is forbidden by local law. For example, a fellow likes to look at pornography, and due to a career need, or family situation, or whatever, finds himself living in a town where pornography is illegal. Under the Fourth Amendment, as written, "...no warrant shall issue, but upon probable cause, supported by oath or affirmation, and particularly describing the place to be searched, and the persons or things to be seized."

So for the guy in the town, as long as he keeps it to himself, there will be no witness, and therefore no oath or affirmation, in turn no warrant will issue. The only way he is likely to run into trouble is if he tries to show, persuade or convert some of his neighbors, and then they can swear out a warrant. This is where the concept from English law comes in, that a man's home is his castle. As long as a person isn't making a public spectacle of non compliance with local law, he or she is sovereign within the confines of his or her own domicile. This concept could easily be extended to sexual lifestyle issues, drug use, and any number of other issues. As we would enter a time of wildly varying local cultures, this use of the 4th Amendment would greatly protect individuals, and yet still allow us to transition to a nation where we all live in communities of agreement. We could live and raise our families in a social environment with which we agreed, and could have a hand in forming.

Another point that should be made at this juncture is that as the years have gone by, many so-called experts have come to agree that the first ten amendments to the Constitution, called the Bill of Rights, should either be applied to just the federal government en masse, or that all ten amendments should be applied to the states, en masse. Neither standard stands up to scrutiny, as each of the first ten amendments, indeed, each of all the amendments, stands on its own, and carries within it instructions as to its application. Thus, while the First Amendment should apply only to the Congress (singular, and therefore the federal Congress) most of the other amendments of the Bill of Rights are clearly intended to apply to the states and localities. Can there be any question that the Fourth Amendment has always been used to prevent unlawful searches and seizures; or that the Fifth Amendment has always been a safeguard against any American having to testify against themselves in any court of the land; or that the Sixth Amendment requires all defendants, even those accused under state or local laws, have a right to a speedy trial? Of course they do, and any attempt to assign application of any amendment to areas not spelled out within the amendment is dangerously disingenuous.

With the wide variety of cultural styles, some of the constitutional limits would come into play. For example, if a community of fundamentalist Muslims formed, honor killings and the cutting off of hands as punishment for theft would both be unconstitutional under the 8th Amendment's prohibition of cruel and unusual punishments. On the other hand, requiring women to wear veils or men to wear beards would be just as legitimate as some other community's requirement that women not go topless.

In the end, with LCMSG up and running, there would be a friendly (or at least non violent) competition between the various communities, with the goal being to determine which belief system produces the most peaceful, contented, healthy, prosperous, and sustainable culture.

The only major concern left to address at this point is national unity. How could such a widely diverse nation be held together? The first answer is that the communication technology would allow us to carry out our natural desire to maintain cultural bonds and/or keep an eye on each other. As some localities found a good way to deal with some health, environmental or industrial challenge, the cultural leaders among us would take note of the advance, and work to adopt it in their own community. So the wise and well meaning leaders among us would always see the reasons to stay united, and have the tools to work toward unity. Maintaining unity across state lines and reducing the excesses of local extremism would be where an involved and imbedded intelligentsia could be most effective (more on this subject in the next chapter), because they could use the cultural tools, such as education, civic and church groups, and other institutions, to bring pressure to bear on those who would oppress.

Beyond open communication, the biggest thing that would keep us being the United States of America would be our mutual love of freedom. Take, for example, the hypothetical case of three soldiers serving together in a combat unit. One is from a secular libertarian town in Colorado, another from a fundamentalist Christian town in Mississippi, and the third from a fundamentalist Muslim town in Michigan.

Even though they might passionately disagree about religion, morals, and how to run society, they could be depended upon to fight together against a common foe, because each knows that when the fighting is over, he or she can return home, where 99 percent of all the aspects of social life is to her or his liking. So while the only thing we might have in common is our love of liberty, the fact that we are allowed to run our own lives the way we want, that mutual love of liberty is enough to get us to stand together against anyone who would threaten that liberty.

This is not just a bunch of theory. The United States of America was originally intended to be different states, with different ways of doing things, united by a common desire for self determination. Our mutual love of liberty has proven to be a bond more than sufficient to keep us united in the past, and would do so again. The proposed transition back to LCMSG is not something new, but rather something old that should be revived. The powers of economic, social, and moral self government used to be held and exercised at the local level, even though it was, admittedly and shamefully, mostly only for white people. But that is the one big thing to which we don't want to return when we revive our historic liberty. There will be more on the subject of race in the next chapter.

For the most part, American communities circa 1850 had the powers of Local Community Moral Self Government, and it served them well. In a process moved by greed, subterfuge, deceit, fear, and apathy, the powers of economic, social, and moral self government were taken from our local communities. Today, bereft of almost any of the real powers of self government, we stand on the brink of falling into an increasingly totalitarian fascism, which our descendants would regret for many generations to come.

Footnotes:

[1.] *Democracy in America* (b), Alexis DeToqueville, (Penguin Books, London, England, 2003), p.805, 806

[2.] *Democracy in America*, Alexis de Tocqueville, 1835, (J.P. Mayer- Ed., Anchor Books, Garden City, NY 1969), p. 68-69

[3.] Ibid, p. 179

[4.] Ibid, p. 70

[5.] *The Forgotten Man, A New History of the Great Depression*, Amity Shlaes, (HarperCollins Publishers, 10 East 53rd Street, New York, NY 10022, 2007) p.346

[6.] Ibid, p.350

[7.] *G.K. Chesterton- Collected Works*, (Ignatius Press, San Francisco, 1987), p. 46

[8.] *Democracy In America*, p.98

[9.] *The Complete Jefferson*, Assembled and arranged by Saul K. Padover, Duell, (Sloan, and Pearce, Inc., NY, NY 1943), p.295

Chapter 5

Racism, Elitism, and Other Considerations

A+B>A

"As for your young men, you call them together and tell them to get out of Washington—tell them to go home, back to the states. That is where they must do their work."

Supreme Court Justice Brandeis, May 24, 1935

Racism

With the basic concept of Local Community Moral Self Government fleshed out, and the realistic and constitutional limits under which it would operate spelled out, there are a number of objections, concerns, and competing ideas to be met before considering how to implement the changes called for.

Probably the biggest objection that will come to the minds of many is that this seems to smack of the old idea of state's rights. On further examination we will see that LCMSG is not only not a call for a return to a racist past, but rather, a way to repair many of the racially based injustices in American history. LCMSG would be a credible and unifying form of reparation.

The major aspect of the African-American experience in common with the experiences of all the other oppressed minority groups in America is that they were all a failure, not of the American concept of liberty, but of the majority of the American people to extend American liberty to all peoples. The minorities all shared to one degree or another, a denial of that American empowerment. Since a denial of American empowerment caused the oppression, a further reduction of that empowerment is unlikely to be the solution.

The experience of African-Americans will be focused on here, not because they are the only minority group to suffer in America, but because the unique extremes of their American experience highlight the negative effects of denying self government to any people. The solutions proposed here to African-American issues are applicable to all groups.

Reparations imply repairing something that is broken. The first thing then is to figure out what is broken, and that will allow us to see how LCMSG will resolve the problem. To be as clinical and unemotional as possible (because this can be a deeply emotional subject) the lasting damage that has been inflicted on the African-American people has been caused by depriving them of the blessings and burdens of free self government in a process that was concurrent with many of the other changes detailed in this book.

Consider the unprecedented depth of the cultural deconstruction that took place during the great African enslavement in the New World. It was a cultural deconstruction so thorough that in many ways African-Americans should be considered a completely new ethnic group on the face of the earth. Each individual African was stripped of almost all cultural accoutrements. First, their clothes were taken and they were forced to accept European styled clothes. Any communication with the old country was impossible. Their language was taken, and they were forced to speak and come to social cohesion in English. Any tribal or national associations were brutally repressed. Nearly all their cultural taboos and markers were lost. Due to the relatively large numbers of slaves brought to work the land, European Americans were diligent in suppressing any expression of African-American identity, unity or self determination.

This experience is unique, certainly in America, and probably, given the size of the enslavement, and the depth of the cultural deconstruction, in the world. The other ethnic groups that came to America, or that were already here, didn't experience this degree of cultural obliteration. The Native Americans, although decimated by disease, murdered on a large scale, cheated and lied to, continued to retain their tribal councils and a degree of national self government and social cohesion.

The Irish, Chinese, and Mexicans, who were probably the most ill-treated of immigrant groups, kept their own clothes, foods, languages, and were still able to keep in touch with their families in the old country. Even in the face of some opposition, they were allowed to associate with one another as they chose. They congregated in their own neighborhoods and in their own towns. After two or three generations, they began to move out into the larger culture, confidently moving forward from a position of strength. This was possible because they had a political and economic power base, due to their being allowed to exercise a great degree of community self government.

There is a consciousness that grows naturally in a group that has any degree of self determination. This consciousness has developed since ancient times in every group in the world. Even in a country as repressed as ancient China, the local warlord demanded tribute, but he left problems concerning water, food, medical care, moral restraint, consequences of immorality, and almost all the other cultural issues, to be worked out by the local villagers. The Chinese saying was that "the sky is high, and the emperor is far away." The same was true in Ireland (where the English rulers took the wheat as rent, and left the Irish to fend for themselves on rotting potatoes), Latin America, and the other areas of Europe and Asia.

Consequently, when these villagers arrived in America, they had a history and a memory of how to run their own communities. Even if they weren't from the same villages, they shared similar systems of taboos, personal responsibilities and expectations, and they knew, without even thinking about it, how to pass these on to their children.

The same was and continues to be true throughout Africa. Africans who were forced on to the slave boats would, if they had been left to their own devices, have been more than capable of forming together in healthy, self governing communities, and would have achieved a strong power base like every other group. Look at the modern experience of the Ethiopian, Jamaican, Nigerian, and other African immigrant communities.

But African-Americans weren't left to their own devices. They were enslaved and their culture systematically suppressed. Since they were legally someone else's property, their wellbeing, in terms of clean water, medical care, food, and shelter, was under the responsibility and authority of their white owners. Even in the area of sexual morality, blacks were encouraged to be promiscuous, as it enabled whites to more easily sell family members for monetary gain, and to engage in selective breeding.

The point is that African-Americans weren't allowed self determination, and therefore weren't forced to respond to the burdens of self government. They were to know their place, do their jobs, and any community problems that arose were to be dealt with by the master in the big house. Usually, the leader of the local black community was the one who could successfully persuade the master to meet some of the community's needs. This happened in the context of what was and is, an entirely new ethnic group on the face of the earth, an ethnic group that has never known self determination.

Things didn't really change much after slavery. There were many in the African-American community who recognized the opportunities and responsibilities inherent in freedom, and worked with courage and enthusiasm to meet them. However, even during Reconstruction, and certainly afterward in the era of Jim Crow, their efforts were thwarted with brutal oppression and terrorism.

Well into the Twentieth Century, African-Americans were kept in near slavery, with no seat at the table where decisions were made. The worst aspect of this, was the fact that the conditions that develop a healthy consciousness of self government were still absent. There were some exceptions to this, in places like Mound Bayou, Mississippi, some towns in Oklahoma, and elsewhere. However, there were too few to change the larger African-American culture.

The issue of lack of cohesion in the black community is long running and well documented. Black on black crime, single motherhood, gangs, drugs, homelessness, and the other symptoms of social breakdown endemic to the inner cities are constantly the subjects taken on by black leaders. It seems African-American intellectuals write and lecture about cultural cohesion more than the leaders of any other group This is completely understandable since social cohesion was taken from them at their genesis, and has continued to be taken from them since. There are clearly many highly moral leaders in the African-American community working on the problem, but the kind of "heart wisdom" in the masses that is community consciousness, can only be raised when a community truly possesses the burdens and options of free self government.

Even with all the obstacles of Jim Crow, African America continued to rise. A business class arose, and black families were becoming stronger and more stable, and the community more cohesive. With the success of the Civil Rights Movement,

African-Americans demonstrated that they had achieved enough strength and influence to gain political equality with whites. Then the great modern tragedy occurred.

Close on the heels of the equalizing Civil Rights and Voting Rights acts (1964-65), Lyndon Johnson enacted a series of socialist programs, called the Great Society. While seemingly well intentioned, these programs continued the crime against the African-American community. They once again denied them the powers and responsibilities of self government. This period, previously referred to as the second metastasizing of the cancer of federal socialism, was the end of almost any community self government for all Americans. The African-American community tragically continued in the status it had from its beginning 400 years previously as a new ethnic group; that of a dependent people with little or none of the powers and responsibilities of self government.

Consider how many cultural decisions used to be made by European-Americans at the local level, and are now made at the federal level; from health care, drug laws, public relief, and moral education of the young, to control of fighting words, and on and on. From 1933 to 1973, a nascent socialism took root in America and fully bloomed in the 1960's, removing almost all the powers of moral self government from all the people, just shortly after African-Americans had gained a real measure of political equality. Truly, the pie turned rotten just as they finally got a piece of it.

Look at the similar cultural effects of these three conditions. In slavery, there was an alienation from the legal structure. The master made the rules, and if one could get away with breaking them, very few of the fellow slaves would hold them to account. As long as what was being done didn't threaten to bring down the master's wrath, it was of no concern to the community because the community hadn't made the rules. That same thinking held true during Jim Crow. The "man" made the rules, so if you could get away with skirting them, more power to you. That thinking was slowly losing ground until the 1960's, but it has come back with a vengeance since then.

"The Man" is back, and these days European-Americans, and everyone else, are in the same boat. Look at how we think today. "We" don't talk about what "we" are going to do to solve a problem. "They" have to solve the problem, and "they" are expected to provide us with all our wants.

We are to do our jobs, and get away with what we can. Whether it's cheating the welfare system, cheating on our taxes, or cheating in traffic, it's only wrong if you get caught. We have no social obligation to one another. If there is any problem, "they" have to solve it. Our leaders are those who can get the master, man, the federal government, to come up with the money to solve our problems for us. It seems this is the mindset of almost the entire country, and it has been termed a "plantation mentality".

The solution to this malady, this almost 400-year-old wound in the African-American community, is the same as the remedy for the ills that affect the entire nation, with all ethnic minorities included. Whether in self segregated or fully integrated communities, the great, historical wound will only be healed through a reinvigoration of Local Community Moral Self Government in this country.

Even some black controlled states won't be the answer if those states are still morally governed from Washington, D.C. The great wounding of African America will end, and the healing begin, when African-Americans are free and equal citizens of self governing communities. This can happen only when most of the powers of self government are devolved from the federal government and back into the hands of state and local governments.

So, is this just advocating a return to "States Rights?" Yes and no, mostly no. First of all, only people have rights, and according to Jefferson, we delegate certain powers to government to secure those rights. This is just saying we should delegate far fewer powers to the federal government, and return most of them to the states and localities. "States Rights" as advocated by those who argued for them, were always about the states being able to deny rights that had already been established, and was therefore, a total lie. The states and the federal government both dropped the ball and didn't honestly enforce the Thirteenth, Fourteenth and Fifteenth Amendments for the nearly 100 years of Jim Crow. This situation has been used in the last forty years to completely discredit local self government, but that is a misreading of history. The federal government was complicit in enabling Jim Crow and therefore, just as guilty as the states.

So the cure for the long-festering wound in the African-American community is the same as the solution to the myriad of problems that afflict every community in America. We must re-establish Local Community Moral Self Government. What's most important is that this time, as we again strive to establish liberty and justice for all, we must be sincere about the "all" part or it simply will not happen.

While we can realistically hope that such a coming together would happen with the restoration of LCMSG, advancing that agenda wouldn't be limited to mere hope. Since the transition to LCMSG would have to be a years long process (more on that in the next chapter) and since America is swiftly becoming a nation with no demographic majority, the minority groups will be in a strong position to scuttle the transition to LCMSG if they become concerned about a racist trend taking hold. This fact will lend a healthy, organic nature to the process.

The concept of self segregation must be mentioned; as free people must be free to self segregate if they so wish. If there could be Black or Hispanic or Asian separatist communities, then White separatism would also have to be allowed. However, even if some wanted to live in that mode, laws still couldn't be written, or rights denied, based on race or ethnicity. If a state were to accommodate some group's separatism, for example by allowing racially conscious contracts, that state would, because of the Fourteenth Amendment, have to accommodate every separatist group. So instead of resembling a melting pot, that state would look more like a checkerboard, with the most extreme separatists having to live cheek by jowl with communities of separatists of other races. That would be delicious irony, and might produce some great football games.

On the other hand, it can be hoped, and frankly, given the mood of the nation and world, realistically expected that most communities would be ethnically diverse. Then we could see communities composed of every kind of human working together and growing together to solve our common problems. Then we could see America advance toward its historic destiny, living out the dream of bridging the planet's ethnic and racial divisions; getting closer to living up to the original national motto of E Pluribus Unum, out of many, one.

Elitism

In looking at the long sweep of American history, and its abuse of minorities, the easy conclusion to make is that we are terribly, perhaps incurably, racist. That would be another misreading of history, because the real culprit has been a long standing, malicious elitism.

From the early 1700's forward, when white and black indentured servants were put into different legal categories, the small group of ruling elites in the South saw that it was in their interests to keep the lower classes of the different races apart. The poor of both races far outnumbered the rich, and if they ever joined forces could easily overwhelm the ruling class, either militarily or politically. The best way to accomplish that separation was to inculcate a virulent form of racism, especially in the minds of the poor whites.

The poor whites were foolish to allow this to happen, but they were after all, also part of an oppressed group. This kind of elitist pitting of ethnic groups against each other went on and spread all over the nation, with Blacks pitted against Whites pitted against Asians, both pitted against Hispanics, Irish against Chinese, Italians against Poles, Asians against African-Americans, and on and on. Mean while, all the various ethnic groups, because of their innate desire to live, were unwittingly pitted against and displacing Native Americans,

So the entire nauseating history of ethnic abuse in American can be laid at the feet of elitist manipulation. The rich and powerful incited racial hatred and interethnic mistrust in order to pit the various groups against each other thereby ensuring and increasing their own wealth. What's more, we can easily see the same kind of thing happening around the world. Raging elitism has been at the heart of most of the world's problems.

The assertion here is (Aristotle to the contrary) there are only two basic forms of government, Local Community Moral Self Government, and the various forms of elitist oligarchy. "Oligarchy" is rule by wealthy families and powerful special interests. Monarchy, dictatorship, aristocracy, Marxism, and the other forms of fascism always seem to have in common that things are actually run by some powerful hidden special interests and wealthy families (oligarchy). The most important aspect of all these other (besides LCMSG) forms of government is that they are all based on elitism, or the idea that some elite group should rule over the rest of us.

The big appeal of this elitism, the thing that legitimizes it in the minds of the participants, is that they think they are so much smarter than the rest of us. That is their big mistake. The basic flaw with elitism can be reduced to a simple mathematical formula, namely A+B>A, where A stands for the wisdom of the elite class, and B stands for the wisdom of all the rest of humanity. This formulation is so important that it is repeated here, in large bold type.

A+B>A

All the mathematical formula A+B>A means is the wisdom and knowledge of all the people together will always be greater than that of any small group of people. It is impossible for it to be otherwise. That small, elite group with all its wisdom and knowledge will always be included in the population as a whole.

Seen in this light, a truly enlightened intelligentsia would not allow itself to be cast in opposition to the people, to rule over them without their consent or understanding. It would instead see their duty in mobilizing and coordinating the wisdom of all the people. That would be the natural, best functioning mode for the elite in a healthy system of government. That was the original way that American society was supposed to operate, with local and state community self government being the vehicle for that mobilization.

Consider how the justices of the U.S. Supreme Court saw things right after they had ruled against the New Deal in the Schechter case in 1935 (detailed in Chapter 3).

"The Supreme Court justices were sending a message to business. McReynolds believed that an unmistakable signal such as Schechter would hearten investors and employers.

But more important was the message they were sending to the White House. Later that day, Justice Brandeis collared the two lawyers who had advised the New Dealers so closely, Tommy Corcoran and Ben Cohen, in the justices' robbing room. Their teacher Frankfurter's suspicion had been correct. The justice told Corcoran: 'This is the end of this business of centralization, and I want you to go back and tell the president that we're not going to let this government centralize everything. It's come to an end.' Brandeis also added a second comment: 'As for your young men, you call them together and tell them to get out of Washington—tell them to go home, back to the states. That is where they must do their work.'" [1]

The work he was referring to was the righting of wrongs, the establishing of justice, and the protection of the downtrodden. It is noble work indeed, but work that can only truly be accomplished by an enlightened intelligentsia working in community to mobilize the wisdom and compassion of all the people. It won't be accomplished by a self anointed elite class ensconced in Washington, D.C. using a distant, unaccountable government to fling out high-minded mandates on a wholesale basis as they conspire to dupe the masses into submission.

You see, what Justice Brandeis was getting at was America was born with, and had inherited from its founders, a system of government far superior to, and far more compassionate than any form of socialism ever conceived. However, since we stumbled into it, our system does not benefit from the systematic defense and articulation that Marxism or any of the other schools of fascism have received.

Marxism and Fascism

To explain that last comment and launch into a defense of the American system, we will take a closer look at Marxism. This examination is appropriate to this manifesto, since one of the goals is to try to tame the runaway beast of the Industrial Revolution. The reason Marxism came into being was an attempt to tame that same Industrial Revolution.

Looking at things from the perspective of early 1800's Germany and Britain, Karl Marx saw societies falling apart because of the ravages brought on by industrialization. Families and communities were being destroyed because machines could make things so cheaply that traditional craftsmen could no longer compete. Marx was not a Luddite, desiring to return to a pre-industrial society, but rather he tried to formulate a way that everyone, and not just the owners of factories, could share in the benefits of the ongoing advance of science.

That original sentiment was admirable, as far as it went. However, in reaching his conclusions that capitalism was the disease, and that the remedy was to have all resources controlled by the government, Marx made two fatal blunders--rejecting capitalism and embracing elitism.

First of all, it is not possible to get away from capitalism. As G.K. Chesterton wrote "If the use of capital is capitalism, then everything is capitalism. Bolshevism is capitalism and anarchist communism is capitalism; and every revolutionary scheme, however wild, is still capitalism. Lenin and Trotsky believe as much as Lloyd George and Thomas that the economic operations of to-day must leave something over for the economic operations of to-morrow. And that is all that capital means in its economic sense."[2]

To see this point from another angle, consider that even a subsistence farmer keeping back some seed corn for next year's planting is a form of capitalism.

Or the same point from yet a third angle. If the most collectivist, "anti-capitalist" society imaginable decided to construct something like a major hydroelectric dam, it could only do so if it had gathered enough resources to provide for thousands of workers for many years. Even if slave labor were used, the slaves would still have to be fed, clothed, and housed. The construction materials and tools would have to be provided, and that process would have to go on for years before the project would begin to yield benefits. That takes a lot of resources in reserve, and that is another name for capital. So what socialism actually is, as Chesterton phrased it, is state capitalism.

Now we return to the main narrative, and identify the second blunder of Marx by focusing on the fact that Marxism is, in fact, state capitalism. Remembering that the definition of Fascism is the combining of big capital with the power of big government against the interests of the poor, working, and entrepreneurial classes, we can see that a Marxist government, which is already a combination of big government with big capital, is always on the verge of becoming fascistic. All it takes is for that government to turn away from benefiting the people and the transition from Marxism to Fascism is complete.

What's more, from the mass starvation of the Ukraine carried out by Stalin to the Maoist purges and the Tiananmen Square massacre in Communist China, such a turning away from benefiting the people is very common in Marxist nations. So basically, Marxism in the real world becomes just another school of real world Fascism.

The mistaken elitism Marx embraced becomes the basis of a bureaucratic oppression that becomes just as bad, or worse, than the capitalist oppression he started out to end. The most likely, but not absolutely certain, way to prevent such a government from turning against the people in that manner is to keep it decentralized and therefore more accountable.

In America, the move toward Fascism has deep roots, beginning early in the 1800's with our national foreign policy of mercantilism. The use of our military and treaty making powers to enhance the profits of American-based corporations was a big step in that direction. This is what the "gunboat diplomacy" of the post Civil War era was about. As Major General Smedley Butler, the first American to be twice awarded the Medal of Honor, said,

"I spent 33 years and 4 months in active service as a member of our country's most agile military force—the Marine Corps. I served in all commissioned ranks from second lieutenant to Major General. And during that period I spent most of my time being a high-class muscle man for Big Business, for Wall Street and for the bankers. In short, I was a racketeer for capitalism. I suspected I was just part of a racket all the time. Now I am sure of it....

I helped make Mexico and especially Tampico safe for American oil interests in 1914. I helped make Haiti and Cuba a decent place for the National City Bank boys to collect revenues in. I helped in the raping of half a dozen Central American republics for the benefit of Wall Street. The record of racketeering is long. I helped purify Nicaragua for the international banking house of Brown Brothers in 1909-12. I brought light to the Dominican Republic for American sugar interests in 1916. I helped make Honduras "right" for American fruit companies in 1903. In China in 1927 I helped see to it that Standard Oil went its way unmolested....Looking back on it, I feel I might have given Al Capone a few hints. The best he could do was to operate his racket in three city districts. We Marines operated on three continents." [3]

That was the way things progressed toward fascism in America's "colonies.' Domestically things went in a similar way, following a path of domestic mercantilism allowed and encouraged after the Civil War. Justice John Marshall Harlan remarked that to keep the nation united we should enter into a kind of "commercial republic." This led the way to corporate personhood, and we were off to the races. NAFTA, the WTO, and other international trade agreements merely extend this concept of a "commercial republic" to the international level. It is a republic in name only. In reality, it is an international fascist oligarchy.

Our national fascism came to adulthood under Franklin Roosevelt, as has been discussed. Any number of specifics could be detailed here, but one of the most apt is to focus on his Council for Economic Development, and the system of farm price subsidies it brought about. These policies literally radically changed the landscape. Prior to these policies, farming was not an enterprise into which corporations entered, because it is too risky. Even in years with a good crop, a farmer might suffer a monetary loss because prices might go down. Consequently, farming wasn't a stable profit-making enterprise, so corporations stayed out of the field. With the federal government guaranteeing high commodity prices, corporations see a likely profit to be made. They will then enter the farming business, driving up the cost of land, and driving out the small farmer.

To understand how much these changes moved us toward fascism, it will be instructive to refer to one of the writings of Alexander Hamilton in "The Federalist Papers", this from "Federalist No. 60"

"...Or, to speak in the fashionable language of the adversaries to the Constitution, will it court the elevation of the 'wealthy and well-born,' to the exclusion and debasement of all the rest of the society?

...I presume it will readily be admitted that the competition for it will lie between landed men and merchants. And I scruple not to affirm that it is infinitely less likely that either of them should gain an ascendant in the national councils, than that the one or the other of them should predominate in all the local councils....

...In a country consisting chiefly of the cultivators of land, where the rules of an equal representation obtain, the landed interest must, upon the whole, preponderate in the government. As long as this interest prevails in most of the State legislatures, so long it must maintain a correspondent superiority in the national Senate, which will generally be a faithful copy of the majorities of those assemblies. It cannot therefore be presumed that a sacrifice of the landed to the mercantile class will ever be a favorite object of this branch of government." [4]

He was arguing that there is a check and balance built into our system in the naturally different interests that lie between the merchants and the farmers. FDR completely undid that natural balance with his program of farm price subsidies, which transformed agriculture into a part of the commercial world, paving the way for Fascism.

Tragically the Industrial Revolution, the taming of which was the goal of Marx, the progressives, and even the industrialists, and which still offers such promise, has been converted during the transition to Fascism into a snarling beast. It ominously threatens to deliver us, with constant surveillance, monitoring and behavior modification, into a totalitarian regime that will keep the fascists in power indefinitely. It is the very promise of technology, if misused to oppress, that makes Fascism so much greater a threat, and therefore so much more to be opposed, than traditional despotism.

Whether referring to traditional despotism or its modern equivalent of Fascism, the aspect which so appeals to the oppressors, is the same aspect that is its fatal flaw-- elitism. For both the captains of industry who want to be free to pursue progress, productivity, and profits, without having to answer to the little people, and the governmental social engineers who know precisely how the minds and culture of the people should be remolded, the idea that the elites should rule over the masses seems as true and natural as the clouds floating over the plains.

This is what can be thought of as the Olympian temptation, the tendency of those who, through talent, drive, ambition, or intelligence have ascended to the top one percent of the population. They think that their accomplishment (or birth) entitles them to ascend the stairway to Olympus, there to commiserate with the other "gods", and rightly decide the fate of humanity.

It's easy to see how someone can fall for this temptation. There will always be a top one percent in any human endeavor. If the top achievers associate mostly with each other, it is easy to think that "we" are just superior to the rest and therefore destined and duty bound to rule them. This temptation is even easier to fall into in the high tech era, if you are one of the elite with the power and productivity of the industrial revolution in your control and not at all controlled by the masses. The great mass of the American people becomes to those elites, just a bunch of food eating breeders living in flyover country.

The tragedy is that to keep this little group in power, there is a concerted effort to prevent the masses from finding any of their own solutions to the problems, or finding a way to community. To keep itself in power, the elite fascist oligarchy uses its power in the media, education, and politics to keep the people divided from each other, and thereby ensure its continued rule, even though it has such small numbers.

In the media; print, broadcast, and internet, the pundits and opinion makers are, almost without exception, basically just mind herders, keeping the minds of the masses firmly stuck in a couple of narrow trenches. This is accomplished by keeping the discussion focused on emotionally charged trigger words, words that most folks will then use, and that can be counted on to provoke an intense response from those on the other side, preventing constructive, honest dialogue even in private conversation.

On the right, the problem is always depicted as overspending by the federal government, too many social programs, and too much intrusion into the marketplace. The inevitable conclusion is that we conservatives must drop all our internal disagreements and vote the Republicans into office in the next election.

On the left, the process is a virtual mirror image. The problem is always depicted as greed, profit, and run away capitalism, with sexism and racism thrown in to broaden the appeal. The inevitable conclusion is that we liberals must drop all our internal debates and get the Democrats elected in the next election. On both sides, anything that doesn't lend itself to simple, sound bite slogans is dismissed out of hand.

Direct involvement with the political parties doesn't typically empower the individual. Inside the organizations of both there is always an urgent need to win the next election, so no time to discuss any other approach or solution. After the election, we are either too busy governing to have a free and open discussion, or nursing our wounds, and regrouping, so there is again no room to explore new ideas.

In this way, a kind of monolithic dichotomy stays in place undisturbed. It's a dichotomy in that there is always just a two-sided discussion. It is monolithic in that individuals must join one side or the other of the two sided debate, and hew faithfully to the entire party line, to have even a slight chance to make an impact. If there is a third way, a way of conciliation, community, compromise, and agreement, it never sees the light of day, and it certainly never makes it onto the planks of either of our major political parties. In this manner, by erecting, maintaining and using the monolithic dichotomy, the elitist fascist oligarchy stays firmly in control.

As a short aside, this is a good place to point out that both sides of our current Fascist oligarchy are basically just materialistic. Even in opposition, the conservatives focus on high taxes, fluid capital, and our material standard of living. Any thought of a more spiritual or moral approach is relegated to the fringes, the cultural conservative camp, which is tolerated but never actually in power. So, in the end, both left and right are merely engaged in a discussion about material good, a dialectical materialism, so it is no wonder that we end up with basically Marxist, or more accurately, Fascist conclusions.

If all this seems to be defining some kind of conspiracy theory, it isn't. Or to be more precise, it isn't referring to a conscious conspiracy. What we probably have here is more akin to the dynamic that can take over in some kinds of card games. Card games in which everyone is in it for themselves, no partners, but in some instances a couple of players have complimentary hands, so they might start leading out with cards that play into the other one's hand, and the tactic is reciprocated in turn. At the end of the hand, those two players have cooperated in helping each other dominate the table, but it wasn't due to a conspiracy. Rather, it grew out of the kinds of cards they were dealt, and their self interested play. Nonetheless, it might look like a conspiracy to the other players.

In the same way, the powerful interests on both the left and the right find it expedient to deal with each other. The big business types want to have corporations run everything, and they are willing to work with the big government types to make that happen. Those who believe in big government want to have a central state rule everything, and they are willing to form common cause with the forces of big capital if that's what it takes to get it done. They might truly despise what each other stand for, but they can get together and share a drink once in a while, and when a toast is called for, what they can agree on is the natural inevitability of a nation controlled by a superior elite class. There are basic forces of greed, desire for power, etcetera, that are built into the psyches of humans These could be working in a negative symbiosis with each other to operate in a way that looks like a conspiracy to those on the outside, just as in the card games illustrated.

Of course, someone who was running a conspiracy to enslave us could use those natural forces to accomplish their goals using a very small band of conspirators. Or such a conspiracy could be rooted in the pits of hell, and using only spiritual forces it would need no other resources to get the job done.

To get a little deeper into the point about conspiracies: It will remain the position of this manifesto that we have merely taken some wrong paths, and need but to return to the right ones. Nonetheless, to be clear on the subject, there might indeed have been a design behind this series of mistakes. There are a couple of specific points in time (besides the entire administration of Franklin Roosevelt, and the traditional whipping boys of conspiracy theorists, like the IRS, and Federal Reserve) where we might see that conspiracy exposed.

The first of these is what has been called the Haymarket Riots, or the Haymarket Tragedy. That event happened on May 4, 1886 at Haymarket Square in Chicago, Illinois. A bunch of radicals and activists were haranguing a crowd. After a couple of hours, a phalanx of police officers moved in to disperse the crowd. This was a fairly typical political activity in the day; much like activists today will block some building and get symbolically arrested, only to be released fifteen minutes later. In those somewhat rougher days, the boys liked to mix it up with the fists a little, but it was all normal political activity.

What happened next was not at all typical. Someone still unknown tossed a stick of dynamite into the advancing formation of policemen, killing seven of the officers. Needless to say, the cops didn't like that, and rioting did ensue. Before the affair was settled, some of the organizers of the rally and some speakers were tried and executed, although no connection to the dynamiter was ever shown.

The way that this might have been part of a conspiracy was that the Supreme Court ruling establishing corporate personhood, *Santa Clara County v Southern Pacific Railroad* came down on May 10th of that year, just days after the incident. So while the nation was just becoming embroiled in what was to be a years long divisive debate about how far labor could go in opposing corporations, the real power of the citizens to charter and control corporations was quietly being usurped in one obscure court case after another. As stated, no one ever discovered who threw that stick of dynamite. It is not impossible that someone who knew what the court was getting ready to do had that stick thrown, as a way of completely distracting the people.

The other evidence of possible conspiracy involves *Roe v Wade* in 1973. At the time, the nation was debating abortion on a state by state basis, but there was no call to legalize it nationally. The reason this ruling might be part of a design is the unique position abortion holds in the philosophical structure of this country. We are founded on the basis of "life, liberty, and the pursuit of happiness". Abortion is the one issue where the right to life might come into conflict with the right to liberty. Whether it does or not depends on when a person thinks life begins.

As such, abortion is an issue that is impossible for a purely American philosophy to solve, and once it was established as a permanent national right by a questionable court ruling, it has become, and will inevitably remain, a source of division in the American mind. There might well have been a design afoot by people smart enough to understand the power of philosophy, to create that kind of permanent division in the American mind. In both these cases we see actions which seem to have no rational motivation that moved the nation toward division and decline.

Nonetheless, all this conspiracy theory stuff is still completely beside the point and non-productive. The only healthy way to look at our situation is to see that for whatever reason, we have taken some wrong turns on the path that have ended us up in a bad place. The thing to do is go back and take the correct path into the future. Continuing on that effort, it will be helpful to look a little closer at the real motivations of those who are running the Fascist oligarchy we are under, and the basic dynamics of its operations.

In the supposedly "free" nations, fascism has a two-sided payoff. (This dynamic is only slightly different in the more openly authoritarian and Marxist nations.) For the captains of big business, the appeal is three-fold. First of all, there is the allure of guaranteed, if not monopolistic markets. This is accomplished by the intertwined relationship between corporate boardrooms and governmental regulatory commissions. Business executives go back and forth, in revolving door mode, helping to write new regulations, which help to shield large corporations from lawsuits and drive smaller competitors out of business. They then go back to the boardrooms where they offer expert advice on how to comply with and evade those same regulations.

The second aspect of the payoff to big corporations is gaining low cost access to resources and raw materials. This is accomplished by implementing government policies, through institutions like the World Bank, IMF, and the Defense Department which strongly encourage leaders of developing nations to approve arrangements to ensure that big corporations have low cost access to their resources.

The third aspect of the payoff of the fascistic system to big business is ensuring low cost labor. Thus, we have a government that encourages outsourcing and off shoring jobs and that can never seem to get a grip on the influx of illegal immigrants. All of these policies favor big capital over the workers and entrepreneurs, but even the supposedly pro-worker politicians don't seem to want to change them.

The other side of the fascist payoff is the one that appeals to the big government types, who mostly think of themselves as liberals, socialists, or progressives. The first aspect of the payoff is that the big capital types donate immense amounts of money to get the big government types elected. This gaining of power is payment in itself, and it enables the progressives to further pursue their larger agenda.

The biggest part of that agenda is the remaking of human culture. From John Dewey in the late 1800's forward, America has suffered under an increasingly powerful, self-anointed elite that considers itself far more enlightened that the rest of Americans, and has taken it as its duty to reform our culture into what they think is best. As such, even though they honestly consider themselves the champions of the downtrodden, they are willing to allow the masses to be degraded even further by the ravages of big business because that will cause us to be more easily controlled and more susceptible to their social engineering.

Consequently, when the corporate masters call for policies that further reduce the status of the American worker, the progressives (and so called conservatives) in power are only too happy to oblige. If this leaves the average worker living hand to mouth, in perpetual debt, and therefore never in economic control of her or his life; having always to work for the corporate masters, that, in the eyes of the progressives (and corporate masters), is good. If those people who can't keep up become wards of the state, so much the better; because then they can be monitored, controlled, and remolded; fulfilling the progressive dream. Moreover, for both the big business types, and the big government types, reducing the power of local community to nothing enables them to pursue every other aspect of their respective agendas with little or no opposition.

With all that said, we are now in a position to attain a very important tool, which is an accurate symbol of modern American fascism. That such a symbol is lacking (the Nazi swastika, connoting so much "German-ness", racism and hatred of Jews isn't apt), like the lack of an agreed upon definition of "Fascism", is a kind of mute evidence that the ruling class knows what it is doing, and doesn't want us thinking about, discussing, or representing it.

The proposed symbol of "Fascism" is a two sided symbol, one for the left face of Fascism, and another for the right face. The left face resembles a backward facing letter "S", with the top half being the hammer and sickle of Marxism, and the bottom half being the bottom of a dollar sign. The symbol of the right face of Fascism is the dollar sign as the top half of the "S" and the hammer and sickle as the bottom half.

This two faced symbol accurately depicts the political agendas of both sides, and will give us a way to represent them. Hence, the cover of this book is a red, white, and blue fist crushing both faces of this symbol, because re-establishing Local Community Moral Self Government will naturally crush both sides of our elitist Fascism, and is the goal of this manifesto.

Consider a couple more thoughts about elitism before setting that subject aside for a while. It isn't wise to assume that some elite group will be honest and well intentioned, because such a system, since it by definition is not as close to or accountable to the community it rules, is more inclined to corruption, power mongering and greed.

Nonetheless, even a well intentioned elitism is still a defective system. Why? Elitism relies on a kind of behaviorism, or Skinnerism (from B.F. Skinner), a doctrine that people can be change psychologically by forcing them to change behaviors. All elite systems suffer from this, because the elite have to be able to control people and force any social and individual changes from the outside in. This is as opposed to the kind of inside out personal change that would be fostered by LCMSG.

With an awareness of elitist use of behaviorism, we can begin to see a truly horrifying specter looming on the horizon. With our increasingly alienated and demoralized populace, that very lack of morality is becoming an issue. Since an entrenched elite class is already in place enthusiastically wielding the tools of behaviorism, if they take it into their heads to raise the moral level of the people, it presents a truly frightening scenario. With the tools of modern high tech surveillance, combined with computer programs such as face recognition technology that can reveal the mental state of the subject, and the vast array of psychotropic drugs, the temptation of those on top to do what it takes to raise our morality, to play god over us, will be irresistible. The horror show depicted in George Orwell's novel "1984" will be a walk in the park compared to where the god players can now take us.

This one point brings into focus the imperative nature of the problem set forth in this manifesto. The only way that the people will regain control over their own government is by a return to Local Community Moral Self Government. Next, it is only by controlling government that we will be able to put the corporate beast back on the short leash of community control. Finally, it is only by attaining a healthy control of corporations that we will be able to get a handle on an out of control industrial revolution.

That industrial revolution, if not controlled by the people for their own good, will be used by the elite to control the masses. The frequent fictional theme of the machines taking over to exterminate the human race misses the real point. The real threat is some group of elites using machines to enslave the rest of the human race. That is what we should, and do, truly fear.

This brings us to the final point about elitism, for the present time. Those on the conservative side, especially those favoring big wealth, like to accuse the opposition of playing "the politics of envy", or being motivated by envy of the rich. There might be some legitimacy to that argument, but not as much as they seem to think.

On the other side of the ledger, the charge should be that those at the top are playing "the politics of self deification", because it seems that many of the elites think themselves to be of a different, divine, nature. Thus, much of their insatiable need to gain power and wealth can be attributed to their desire to demonstrate their own divinity to themselves, if not to others. With that in mind, it is urgent that we realize that we are dealing with some deluded megalomaniacs, some of the big business/big government types (fascists) who have seized control of the industrial revolution and who view themselves as gods. They therefore have no upper limit to their self serving schemes for humanity. They will stop at nothing and must, therefore, be stopped by the rest of us.

The sad thing is that so many of us are so willing to be ruled over and become wards of the state or wage slaves. This is probably due to two factors. Historically most humans have preferred some kind of slavery over the duties of free people (more on this subject in the next chapter). Also, modern work itself has become drudgery–filled and soul-numbing.

The alienated nature of modern work is widely lamented, but we haven't focused enough on the possibility that over centralized corporations make that alienation inevitable. Corporations seem to be dedicated to taking all the control from the workers, and doing everything they can to take more than their share of the fruits of that work. So if we feel used and demeaned, we should. If some of us instead choose to live on a government dole, who can blame us? Thus, the elites that would rule over us have created a self-fulfilling prophecy. They think of us as food eating breeders living in fly over country, and so we are becoming.

Little Freedoms

Consequently, most Americans are either exploited, oppressed or both. The benefits and joys of free life, where we can live much more how we want, enjoy the fruits of our labors, have more free time, and have much more control of how we spend our wealth, time and labor are lost to our minds. Tragically, also lost to us is the sheer joy of working and the feeling that we are contributing to the good of ourselves, our families, and our communities.

It doesn't have to be this way. Many have dreamed and written about the promise of the industrial revolution, but the worldwide turn toward socialism has exacerbated, rather than solved the problem. Well meaning revolutionaries of the past and present have not only missed the problem of corporate personhood, but they also don't see that "capitalism" *per se*, isn't the problem. Rather, runaway elitism in the form of greed and power mongering is the problem, and it is not avoided through socialism.

It was mentioned earlier in order to keep themselves in power, the elites use their power to keep the people divided. They accomplish that quite well, and have also taken from our lives, and our minds, the kinds of community and personal options given to us by nature to solve problems. We are left thinking that only big government/big business solutions are possible. To begin to see how LCMSG might bring about a world enjoying the full benefits of technology, we will start by looking at an excerpted, earlier quote form DeTocqueville.

"Thus, I think that the type of oppression threatening democracy will not be like anything there has been in the world before;...

Above these men stands an immense and protective power which alone is responsible for looking after their enjoyments and watching over their destiny. It is absolute, meticulous, ordered, provident, and kindly disposed. ...It provides their security, anticipates and guarantees their needs, supplies their pleasures, directs their principal concerns, manages their industry, regulates their estates, divides their inheritances. Why can it not remove from them entirely the bother of thinking and the troubles of life?

Thus, it reduces daily the value and frequency of the exercise of free choice; it restricts the activity of free will within a narrower range and gradually removes autonomy itself from each citizen

It does not break men's wills but it does soften, bend, and control them; rarely does it force men to act but it constantly opposes what actions they perform; it does not destroy the start of anything but it stands in its way; it does not tyrannize but it inhibits, represses, drains, snuffs out, dulls so much effort that finally it reduces each nation to nothing more than a flock of timid and hardworking animals with the government as shepherd." [5]

As though in echo to DeTocqueville, and to see how far down that path we have traveled, consider the following passage from "The Death of Common Sense":
By Phillip K. Howard,

"They miss the problem entirely. Our hatred of government is not caused mainly by government's goals, whatever their wisdom, but by government's techniques. How law works, not what it aims to do, is what is driving us crazy.

Freedom depends at least as much on deciding how to do things as deciding what to do. Thousands of rigid rules are not needed to satisfy the important goal of worker safety; people could come up with their own plan, as Glen-Gery Brick did, and do a much better job. Our "primary concern," Professor Larry Preston has suggested, "should be to create arrangements that support our freedom to choose."

Law is hailed as the instrument of freedom because without law, there would be anarchy, and we would eventually come under the thumb of whoever gets power. Too much law, we are learning, can have a comparable effect: Millions of tiny legal cubicles give humans virtually no leeway. Unlike any legal system we ever admired, it tells us what to do and exactly how to do it.

It is no coincidence that Americans feel disconnected from government: The rigid rules shut out our point of view. Americans feel powerless because we are not given a choice: Modern law does not allow us, to quote Justice Cardozo, "to complete and correct the rigidity of instruction by the suppleness of instinct." [6]

Where is this train of thought taking us? DeTocqueville warned of the totalitarian tendencies of democratic governments, and how they would take from the individuals the ability to do things for themselves. Howard shows how far we have already gone in that direction.

In all of this the concept of liberty or freedom looms behind the scene. Liberty has mostly come to denote the freedom of the greedy to take as much as they can, that is freedom in a large, centralized sense. What is missing is the kind of freedom in the small community or individual sense, the lack of which is warned by DeTocqueville and bemoaned by Howard. But it is that very small scale freedom, with its flexibility and responsiveness which could help to bring about the promised day of technology truly benefiting the planet.

To develop this concept so that we can begin to realize the kind of problem solving little freedoms which have been lost to our minds, we will consider how freedom could help to solve some of our current problems. Keep in mind that the following is a list of suggestions, merely some of the solutions that could come up if we were free to govern ourselves in our own communities. When Robert Kennedy was laid to rest in 1968, his brother Edward eulogized him as someone who, unlike others who look at things and ask "why?", would look at possibilities and ask "why not?." The following proposed solutions fall under the general rubric of "why not?" with the constant answering refrain being, "Because we are not really free."

The first problem to approach is homelessness. Most of us think that the reason for homelessness is that some folks just can't make it in society, so they fall through the cracks and become homeless, needy and dependent. However, it will surprise most people to be informed that the biggest reason for homelessness is simply the lack of low cost housing, and the biggest reason for that shortage is zoning laws and financing policies which prevent the construction of such housing.

So, the suggestion is that we (government?) allow not subsidize very small housing, housing of a type that could easily be expanded by the owners. This type of housing could be called "micro-incremental" housing. It would enable a low paid worker to actually own a small (5'x 8') dwelling with the wages that could be earned in just a few weeks or months. Then, if the worker continued to work steadily and live frugally, he or she could expand the dwelling in small increments. In the course of just a few years, the diligent, frugal worker could own a one bedroom house, and have built that equity without having gone into debt. The technology involved could range from factory-made modular units of pre-stressed concrete, steel, or plastics to low-tech options like hay bales or rammed earth. And there is literally no telling what other innovative systems would come up, if the lower wage earner were free to innovate.

Imagine how revolutionary such a change could be, with the little people being able to build equity without going into debt. If the current homeless population were allowed that freedom, it wouldn't be long before the young just leaving school and entering adult life would demand the same freedom, and before long most people would build equity and wealth that way, without becoming indebted.

All that would be required would be an easing of some of the zoning laws. Some property owners would be more than happy to allow some small, new development on their land. The zoning restrictions would have to be changed first, and that might arouse the opposition of those who feared the lowering of their own property value. So maybe these kinds of micro incremental housing developments would be restricted to certain zones, but even then the poor would be benefiting from the kind of freedom that used to prevail in this nation.

Just a few asides before we go to the next societal problem that could be at least partially solved by a judicious application of liberty. For the most part, zoning laws came about through the encouragement of the federal government. During the 1930's, the feds went around demolishing shanty towns, what they termed sub standard housing. While it must be admitted that some zoning laws are necessary for the protection of the health of the community, the tendency of the zoning laws has been to go too far, and to start mandating minimum square footage, expensive building materials, etc. This has brought about an artificial bottom to the price of housing, with the sentiment being that we want to protect and increase property values. This use of the hand of government, socialism in a sly form, to benefit the already wealthy, could be considered another definition of Fascism. What started with the sentiment that "people can't be allowed to live like this" (in sub standard housing) has resulted in millions of people living on the streets, in public shelters, or in prison cells.

What's more, we can see at this point how Fascism generates its own local franchises. The zoning laws, development plans, and banking policies, all supported by the federal government, create an artificial dearth of low cost housing, and those who suffer homelessness as a result come to be another group of wards of the state. In the end, the few profiteers on top immensely increase their wealth and social engineers get more lives to mold.

It would be healthier and fair to allow a little freedom, so that the working poor could build and buy the kind of housing they could afford. These same folks, who perhaps have some personal emotional problems, would be enabled to deal with their problems in the freedom and space of their own homes, and rebuild themselves into the people they desire to be, rather than what some social worker thinks best.

One short note is in order. If we did go the route of micro incremental housing, it would greatly lower the cost of all housing (the immutable law of supply and demand). The result would be a lower cost of living, which in turn would enable this nation to attract low cost manufacturing back to these shores. This kind of judicious application of liberty, even if on a local small scale, could have large, macro-economic effects.

In the novel "Babbit" Sinclair Lewis exposed the local political machine in the fictional "Zip City" of the 1920's. The real estate developers and bankers made great profit selling tracts in the new section of town. They then used those profits to buy new land even further out, and to get their own candidates elected to the city council. The city council then decided to extend city services (water, roads, sewage, electricity) in the direction of the new development. This greatly increased the value of the land being developed, making it easy to sell at a great profit, which was then re-invested.

In the modern era, this kind of political machine continues to thrive and is the basis of homelessness with one major addition, that of the automobile. Space for automobiles is mandated by zoning laws for every new business and dwelling. Our cities are built in such a way as to keep us addicted to cars and petroleum. This brings us to the subject of transportation.

When the discussion turns to transportation, we generally think in terms of the private automobile, and the subsidized mass transit system. This is a gross misunderstanding of our actual situation. Our real mass transit system is the private automobile and it is greatly subsidized. From local, state and federal taxes going to build highways, streets, bridges, traffic lights and other controls, and the safety, emergency and police resources dedicated to our mass transit system, those who don't own automobiles pay a lot to support those who do. This is beside the fact that most merchants and housing developments are mandated to supply parking facilities which non drivers and drivers support. What's more, the owners of the autos pay large sums of money for the vehicles, as well as gas, maintenance and insurance. All of this money, public and private, is necessary because our mass transit system, the nominally private auto, is the most inefficient mode of transportation imaginable. For the normal individual to go out to merely get a cup of coffee, he or she must move about three thousand pounds of metal along with them.

This dubious situation was brought about shortly after World War II by a questionable interaction of big business and big government. There is a lot of evidence that General Motors, or some affiliate holding companies, systematically bought up and deconstructed the existing streetcar systems. (Google "The Great American Streetcar Scandal") These systems were converted to buses and since have been openly subsidized by the federal government, and mandated to be inefficient and slow.

The resulting inadequate public transit system in almost every American city generally results in the low paid worker having to own an automobile in order to hold a low paying job. Most manufacturing jobs are now located on the fringes of our cities, where land is cheap, and the buses don't run. Or they don't run in that area at the times of night those entry level workers must work. So they must buy a car, which in turn drives up the wages they must earn, making the United States less attractive to international manufacturing, as well as greatly congesting our highways.

Instead of trying to tweak federal transportation policy to solve some of this problem, the little freedom market-based solution would be to legalize a form of mass transit that is very popular and effective in other nations known as the jitney cab. A jitney is different from the normal cab in that a jitney can have multiple riders going to various locations. Ever present in some third world countries, jitneys are always available. You flag one down going in the general direction you want to go, and quickly negotiate with the driver how much it will cost to take you to either your destination or a major cross street. You pay the driver, get in, and join a number of other riders on their way to their locations. As the jitney goes along, some folks get off, and others get on,.

In our high tech nation, this basic operation could be improved with cell phones and computer dispatching. The cost to the individual rider would be almost as cheap as present day buses, and the door-to-door service it offers would be nearly as convenient as the private vehicle. We could easily conceive of subscriber commuter service, a kind of commercial car pool, to and from downtown jobs, or commuter rail stations, and homes. Shopper services and the like could also come about. Low paid workers could get to and from low paying jobs, at any time of the day or night, with much less out of pocket expense. As a result, we might attract more low paying jobs. For every jitney (think 15 passenger vans) on the freeway, the result would about be ten fewer cars. With a multitude of jitney companies operating, the system would provide a major reduction in traffic congestion and lower highway construction and maintenance costs. A larger scale transit system could grow in an organic, free market way, as jitney companies replaced 15 passenger vans with larger buses on busy routes.

All these benefits could come to us with a system of multiple jitney companies up and thriving. Not only would some government subsidy not be required, but it would allow us to end subsidies to both so-called mass transit as well as many of the subsidies to highway construction and other aspects of the private auto system. So you might ask, since this is such a good idea, why hasn't it risen naturally in our free market system? For the most part, jitney cabs aren't legal in most cities in this nation. Simply put, it is because we aren't free, in that meaningful, small sense of freedom.

This is so, even though that kind of freedom would create many jobs, especially for the poor in the inner cities, and it would also help to reduce the problems associated with pollution. But let's face it, the present system sells cars and oil, and enhances the multi-national corporations immense freedom to be greedy. At the same time, the problems of pollution and climate change are becoming an increasingly strong rationale for imposing the controls of big government into our private lives. The big government types argue it seems a system of private freedom hasn't been able to solve the problem.

The next subject to be considered is the perpetually controversial subject of health care. This issue best crystallizes the absolute necessity to return to Local Community Moral Self Government, and the small, personal freedoms to be found there. Health care is a priceless service we all need, and one that in time of crisis, we will pay any amount of money to receive (for either ourselves or our loved ones). As such, if priceless health care is put in the hands of distant corporations, it will inevitably become a vehicle for runaway greed, and will bankrupt us as individuals. Since greed knows no upper limits, and if greed is the guide, many of the needy among us will never receive adequate care.

On the other hand, if health care is put under the control of distant, centralized government, it will probably become the leading edge of totalitarianism. Once personal lifestyle decisions are connected with the federal budget, the logic will inevitably grow that in order to keep costs manageable, government officials (who will probably be exempt from the controls) will be empowered to control an ever increasing portion of the lives of the masses.

The solution to this health care dilemma is to choose the third way, the way of local community. On the level of local community, individuals have the primary focus of their identity based on their place in the community. Health care becomes more of a calling, and the community is empowered and behooved to address the health needs of the entire community. The thinking is that if health needs, particularly of the poor, are ignored, it effects the well being of the whole community. Therefore, the whole community must respond to those needs.

Obviously, we won't arrive at that kind of community based thinking regarding medical care if we move in that direction only regarding medical care. We can't expect health care workers to have that high and generous consciousness if the rest of society is selfish and uncaring. It can only be arrived at in a society where we all have our primary identity based on our place in the community. With the re-establishment of LCMSG, this could happen.

Add to that the fact that these same local communities would have the power to legislate against unhealthy behavior and educate the young about morality in ways unavailable at the present time. We can see that this improved architecture of government could successfully deal with the challenges of health care. What's more, with a vibrant community spirit aroused, clinics and other institutions could be organized to aid the poor.

More to the point of this section, once we put the responsibility for health care in the hands of local community, there would be many small freedom ways we could improve health care. If the restrictions of the 1905 federal Food and Drug Act were removed, we, as free local communities, could license health care workers, and allow the sale of medications according to our own standards, and not according to cost increasing, option reducing federal standards. This would involve other medical schools besides AMA schools, and access to low cost medicines, alternative and herbal remedies, medicines from other countries, or even going without the present system of prescriptions.

One particular case will fill in some of what is being proposed here. When a person has a crown on a tooth, it is cemented into place. When it comes loose, a person has to go back to a dentist to have it replaced. The cost can be from free (from a friendly dentist who recently installed the crown) to thirty to a hundred and fifty or more dollars. Then the dentist cleans out the crown and tooth of old cement, puts in fifty cents worth of new cement, and puts the crown back in place. The question is why can't the cement be available for the general public to purchase, and apply at their own risk? Once again, the sorry answer is that we are not that free. The cement to replace crowns on teeth is not available for sale to the general public.

There are any number of other medical issues that could be affected by an increase of small freedom. They include cancer drugs from Mexico to low cost alternatives from Canada and Europe. And we can play a long game of "why not?' around the issues of health care such as why can't we all, as patients, have a personal USB drive, (or whatever memory device comes along) and use it to carry all our personal information. Go to a doctor for a checkup, and the doctor downloads all new information to your drive. Get an x-ray, or MRI, or any other diagnostic procedure, and that information gets put onto the drive. Then you can go to any other provider and give your own information to them, without having to undergo new tests. You could shop around for your own tests, procedures, or second opinions.

Or, why can't we go to a diagnostic kiosk at a Walgreen's-tm, CVS-tm or other drug store, answer some questions, maybe hook up to a blood pressure machine, and get an opinion about which drug to take, or a referral to a specialist ? Those kinds of machines could even be owned by private individuals in their own homes. Then, we could go buy the drug, at our own risk, or go to the referral, possibly via video. All of this would greatly reduce costs, restore options to the individuals, and probably enhance the health of the nation.

But of course, all this freedom would reduce the cash flow to the health care corporations, and also reduce the power of the federal government. It is very interesting and instructive to look at how the federal government has dealt with the issues of health care over the long term. First, they greatly reduced the health care choices available to the people in 1905, and then, a few decades later, that same federal government began to provide health care to the masses. Then, when times of budget stress come and health services are consequently reduced, the people clamor, to the point of becoming violent, in calling for even more federal intervention in health care. So the authorities that took away free choices and options get the victims of their restrictions to demand they be given even more power. Thus goes the spiral of a declining nation.

In the end, health care is a great example of why a community based approach to issues is far superior to an elite, top down approach. On the local level we can risk allowing solutions based on personal freedom, because we will be dealing on a person to person basis. Moral persuasion would return to its proper, crowning place in human community. Cultural leaders would work to influence their neighbors in dealing with the issues of smoking, obesity, and other destructive habits. Care can be provided in a much less expensive and personal way.

If everything is on the distant elite level, it will be much more mechanical and legalistic. Instead of working to morally persuade free individuals, the on high elites merely issue mandates, and consider the problem solved. This can leave many to suffer in silence, and might create an underground economy of those who aren't persuaded. In addition, the thinking about what is the best for all can easily, if made behind closed doors by an "enlightened" elite class, become a corrupt, politically driven thinking.

All of this emphasizes the principle that the natural elite that we will always have, whether of medical professionals or any other field, must be involved within the community, not ruling over it. That can only happen if we are all involved in community, and have our primary identity as community members, and not as consumers, workers, owners, or professionals.

Another area in which the people could be greatly benefited by creative application of little freedoms is education. For the most part, the issue of education is always raised with the intention of getting even more funding, usually from the federal government. The truth is that America spends more money per pupil than virtually any other nation, with far less to show for it. As we launch into this issue, the first question must be, "How can education, which is basically the impartation of information, become such an expensive problem in this age of hi-tech information?" The short answer is that this is another example of the great advances of science and the industrial revolution being used by the elite to control, not benefit, the masses.

One of the ways education could be freed up for the people is to look at all the occupations that require a government license. We could ensure if there is a test to get a license, the information being tested is available, on line and/or through the public library, in the form of interactive educational programs at no cost to the public. People with the drive and discipline to get through the programs could pay a reasonable test fee, get a license, and begin practicing their occupation.

In the same way, if some local industry found itself becoming obsolete due to changing technology, the workers, using this kind of education system, could be inexpensively re-trained for the next wave of technology. If someone wanted to benefit from the discipline and guidance of a more traditional educational approach, with teachers, classrooms and such, that would still be available (probably, due to supply and demand, at much less cost), but even those students would have to pay a fee to take the government licensing test.

Another way that our hi-tech information capability could be used to benefit the masses would be in the field of entertainment. It is simply a fact that most of the young can't name the presidents, tell you which century the Second World War was fought, or how the Constitution is supposed to be used. They can tell you all about how to text, tweet, or the latest scandal with the latest pop star. This leads to a lot more "Why nots?"

Why not have the entertainment shows teach actual history, science, law, etc. This wouldn't have to apply to all shows, or impede artistic license, but could involve some sort of authenticating authority, or free market institution issuing a seal of authenticity. The authentication would be displayed at the beginning and end of the program declaring that the historical, legal, scientific, or whatever information contained therein is approved as being accurate and true. Parents could look for that seal, and be assured that they and their children are learning things considered true, and would be taught as such in schools. The same method could be used in video and computer games, so those tremendous potential tools of education could actually be used to educate.

Many will object at this point that this will require the intervention of big government and therefore violate the most basic premise of this manifesto. This then becomes a good moment to further develop how LCMSG and its system of little freedoms could work. There might at times be legitimate reason to use the heavy hand of government, maybe even the federal government (by amending the Constitution). Some problems might have to take that approach. But it would always be the case that we should prefer to not use the heavy hand of central government. We are always trying to preserve that local mind of government, and the positive morality inducing feedback loop between government and the individual. For the most part, such government intervention would best be used in abeyance, as a standing threat looming over the scene, an option we could use, but would prefer not.

When we went as a united community to some Hollywood production company, and informed them that we would love to see them produce shows with the aforementioned authenticity, the producers would be looking at a very persuasive argument. If they concurred and took a little more effort to comply with the requirements of authenticity, they would win much good will, and incidentally, sell a lot of movies and games. If, on the other hand, they refused out of ignorance or some other base motivation, the community could resort to the heavy hand of government. The producers would still have to either produce that kind of entertainment, or let some others and they would have gained the lasting antipathy of the community. For the most part, the community will could prevail on the free market, and the heavy hand of government would remain unused.

The next issue that will be explored as we focus on the potential benefits of LCMSG and the small freedoms it enables will be corporations, industrial policy and labor relations. Noted activist Erin Brockavitch, subject of the movie which bears her name, was heard to comment that most corporations know the right thing to do, and would do it, but there is no motivation in the board rooms except that of greed. Returning to pre-corporate personhood days, to a time when corporations were chartered at the local and state level, would change that situation, and ensure that a voice of holistic community benefit was heard in the board rooms.

This would involve far more than just large scale environmental damage or unsafe work practices. In this day and age, every time the federal government passes new mandates, like requiring health insurance of full time workers, most companies put all the workers on a part time status, and dodge the law. Companies routinely have changing shifts, short hours, systematic layoffs followed by rehire at lower wages, and a host of other ways to harass and exploit workers.

At the same time, companies will sue those who stand up at public hearings in opposition to some new store or development. The company will claim its ability to do business is being threatened by the individual citizen speaking up. Even though the company knows it will eventually lose in court, it sues anyway, because it loses only if the individual can and will dedicate enough time and money to win. Most won't, so opposition to corporate policy is silenced.

If corporations had to answer not just to courts and legislators, but to the more nebulous but thorough standard of community benefit, most of this kind of underhanded manipulation would end. If corporations had to perpetually answer the question, "How is this enterprise benefiting the community that is granting you the charter to do business?" these kinds of family and community destroying practices would be a thing of the past.

Another aspect of industrial policy that would find better resolution with LCMSG in place would be that of merit pay. In today's world, unions almost always resist merit pay, the concept by which people are paid according to the quality and/or quantity of their work. The unions resist for the good reason that companies have often used merit pay in a low, manipulative way to simply divide workers against each other, setting up things like contests that reward the worker that produces the most. Usually, such contests create a major increase in productivity, and the one worker who wins the contest actually gets a fair reward, while all the others get nothing.

Unions insist on no merit pay, but then the only basis for promotions and raises is longevity. This leads to mediocrity and time serving. If your work is superior, there is no reward, and if your work is inferior, there is no loss, unless it is bad enough to warrant termination.

LCMSG would improve this situation. It would enable corporations to engage in merit pay, which would greatly improve our work ethic and attract new industry. We could safely do so, because companies would be hesitant to abuse merit pay because they would be on the short leash of community accountability. Taking us away from the present legalistic standards would allow us to avoid both extremes. Merit pay could be allowed, but with the concept of benefiting community, we would have the language to define abuse, and the power to limit it. At the rounder, more nuanced, table of LCMSG, both sides can be addressed, and the community benefit of merit pay can be accomplished without risking abuse.

If most industrial policy is set at the local level with the power to charter corporations, the effect would be more than just how we regulate business. Since that local mind would have to wrestle with the entire range of challenges facing all human communities, it would not only seek to protect the well being of citizens, but would also work to infuse a strong work ethic and morality of personal honesty, so that local companies could compete in the larger world. Thus, installing these powers at the local level would benefit all members of the community.

In all of the cases highlighted here, from homelessness to industrial policy, the proposed solutions will get traction only at that round table of LCMSG. If the issues continue to be controlled in Washington, D.C., we can expect the influence of big corporations in the cases of industrial relations, transportation, housing, professional organizations regarding medical care and education, unions regarding education, transportation, and industrial policy to continue to dominate. The innovative solutions that are possible don't even come up, let alone get acceptance, when money and influence control the game. And we continue to be hamstrung by the mistaken notion that only big centralized solutions can work.

At the round table of LCMSG many of these ideas, and an unknown multitude of even more innovative ideas, could be heard and win acceptance. It is so much harder to deny someone a simple freedom that might be to their benefit when you are sitting in the same room, looking that person in the eye. Then, when some social service must be cut due to a lack of funds, the one being threatened with reduced benefits has a great deal of credibility when asserting that they could make their own way if not burdened by controls and regulations designed to keep others rich. On the other hand, with those little freedoms available to all, those who don't achieve prosperity would have less of a claim on our sympathy and relief, and those who do gain our sympathy would do so on a case by case, humane basis.

This brings us to one of the big points of this manifesto, which is that we simply have to re-think the industrial revolution. The heart of the problem is that efficiency and profit are now the only guides of industry and corporations. So the move is always toward automation, robotics, and outsourcing and off shoring labor. If this results in fewer and fewer jobs, so much the better for profit, even if it decimates the population. This paradigm is not sustainable, fair, or even sane.

The thinking that can solve this problem has to start at the local level, in the minds of local communities and citizens, and putting corporations in their place as creations of and part of the community. With Local Community Moral Self Government, we would have the language and the tools to address the problems that have developed with the industrial revolution.

So what kind of re-thinking of the industrial revolution is called for? Thankfully, the modern world and our own history provide some examples. In Japan, there is almost no governmental welfare system, and the major corporations are expected, as good citizens, to provide small, low skilled jobs to low skilled and disabled workers. So you have the case of a person with a low I.Q. working on an assembly line, putting apples into little net bags. Apples cost a little more because of it, but in Japan, everyone can have the dignity of having earned their own way in life.

Modern Germany has also taken a small step back from complete efficiency, to emphasize closer to full employment. No doubt they could be more efficient, but they reason that in the long run, such inhuman efficiency hurts the community, the culture, and the economy.

Our American past also provides an example. In the South before the Civil War, states put some inefficient controls on the railroads. Lines could only run from one city to another, and freight had to be transshipped by workers from one line to another. In addition, there were some requirements that each rail line had to be of a different gauge, so the lines couldn't be easily consolidated. This all made things somewhat less efficient (they probably still benefited from 90% of the greater efficiency of rail over horse drawn freight) but it ensured workers still had work, and it kept the owners of the new technology of the time, railroads, from getting so much wealth that they could seize control of the political process.

The industrial revolution has to be re-thought, and it might involve getting some international government agencies involved in things like the environment. It might involve some national agencies. Nonetheless, the consciousness of seeing corporations, and the industries they control, as part of the community with an obligation to serve the good of the community, starts at the community level with the reinvigoration of LCMSG, even if some of the conclusions might lead to the national and international level. In the end, most of the regulations that domesticate corporations and the industrial revolution will be generated at the local level, making local, human sized accommodations between workers, owners and citizens.

It is not impossible for us to get to that world that is greatly benefited by the industrial revolution. It must begin with our willingness to re-think and domesticate it. We might decide to get away from this consumer based economy, one that turns out goods so shoddy that we must work long hours to afford shoddy replacements, thus keeping the economy churning and generating huge amounts of waste. Instead, we could produce solid, long lasting and repairable products. This would reduce the amount of work, and automatically ease humanity's impact on the environment.

To make such a system work, we might go to a twenty hour work week, with each job paying enough for a person to actually build a life. We might even have to allow some slight inefficiency into the system to reach these ends, but let's keep in mind how much inefficiency in areas like housing, transportation, medical care, education, etc., are presently put in place, often by government regulation, for the purpose of enriching the already wealthy.

In the entire discussion on this subject, we would want to hold on to the idea that technology, corporations, and government are intended to serve humanity, and we have a right to demand they do so. At the same time, we should work diligently to preserve our system of private, free enterprise, with the many benefits it brings. Most can be taken care of by a return to LCMSG, and the healthy community mind it will generate. History has proven the most likely way those benefits will come to us is if we have enough community control over that market to ensure that it remains free, and doesn't slide into monopoly, collusion or other forms of corruption.

It has to be emphasized that LCMSG will be business friendly, especially when compared to big socialism. With LCMSG, businessmen will not be the enemy or the exploiter of the masses. Nor will it be the subject of never ending regulation and scrutiny by the federal government. They will be sort of working class heroes, necessary and appreciated members and pillars in a healthy community. Private enterprise, with the restraint of community, can be the best conceivable system, but to do so requires empowered communities that can think about and enforce chartering policies requiring corporations to benefit the community.

Another point from the past should be made, one that relates back to the labor unions. In the early Twentieth Century, a time of monopolies and progressives, a labor organization appeared called the Industrial Workers of the World or IWW for short. Those who went around advocating for the IWW were called "Wobblies" and one of their favorite themes was they thought if the workers of America would form one big union, that they could bring the bosses to their knees. What they didn't realize was that before corporate personhood, when corporations were dependent on state and local governments to get chartered, we basically had one big union (of all citizens) in this country. One again, it is a shame no one at the time realized what had actually happened, and what had been lost.

The Third Way

In the book, "The Greening of America" a somewhat premature homage to the culture-changing power of the 1960's "Counter Culture" Charles A. Reich makes the point that there is a Consciousness I, Consciousness II, and Consciousness III. [7]

Consciousness I is basically the conservative position that the invisible hand of the free market will bring about the best society. As we have seen, while there is a great validity to some of that reasoning, a lot of it is rendered irrelevant because with the advent of corporate personhood and the monopolies that followed, that invisible hand of the free market no longer operates.

Consciousness II is basically that of the New Dealers, and their descendants. That position holds that the market will only deliver great benefits to society if it is controlled by the heavy hand of the distant, powerful federal government. Their challenge is to come up with the perfect set of government regulations to get to that better world. We have seen how those good intentions, when tried in the real world, become the tools of the elite. We have ended up under the thumb of a very subtle, two faced form of Fascism, what Reich terms the "corporate state".

Consciousness III, as defined by Reich, is beyond and apart from either of the first two, which have landed us in that corporate state. It is much more based on consciousness than on any legalistic formula or political platform. He proposed that this "revolution by consciousness" would be the way to a new revolution, and would change the political forms as one of its last acts. Perhaps he was correct, and hopefully the thinking of the masses has risen to the point where they can see that LCMSG can be the vehicle for a greater growth in consciousness, and the form a new political change can take.

Local Community Moral Self Government certainly corresponds to the third way of thinking that many are calling for, but there is another era from our past that fills the same role, and is largely forgotten to our minds. The Victorian Era is remembered, if it is remembered at all, as a time of strict and stifling moral codes, and narrow gender roles. While some of that is true, most of those aspects of Victorian thinking wouldn't have to be reborn for us to regain the advantages of Victorian thinking.

Queen Victoria launched the social reforms named for her as a response to the social breakdown of the early industrial revolution in Britain. She saw young people from the countryside being forced by big landowners consolidating the land, into the cities to become workers in the factories. The young men and women could hold the backbreaking jobs for as long as their health held up, and then they were forced into the "workhouses", or church sponsored homeless shelters of the day. Even when working, the young men didn't make enough to support families, and so most remained single. The young women fared even worse.

Human nature being what it is, the men still sought the comfort of a woman's arms, and the women, having little work or money, were willing to comply for a price. Consequently, the streets of British cities were full of homeless men, prostitutes and single mothers, surrounded by herds of nearly orphaned urchins. Family breakdown, crime, and disease were rampant.

The Victorians waded into this mess with a number of initiatives. First, they called on the captains of industry to pay a "family wage" whereby one man could earn enough to support a family. At the same time, pressure was placed on developers to build small family dwellings, and to make the rest of the plan work, women and children working in the mines and factories started coming into disfavor.

As the plan developed women were expected to work only until married, and then to stay home and take care of the children. That, along with taking children out of the factories, greatly reduced the number of available workers and due to the immutable law of supply and demand, factory owners were forced to pay a family wage to attract adult male workers.

In addition, a strong moral component, coming from the churches and schools, encouraged monogamous, stable marriages, and the entire social compact was formed. That latter part is the only part of the Victorian agenda we remember today, and that is the one that could be most easily modified to accommodate some of our new thinking about family. It wouldn't have to be only women who stay home, or only men who went out of the home to work, but along with concessions from business, it probably would involve some voluntary earning restraint, and some moderation of our consumer appetites on the part of upstanding citizens.

For the most part the Victorians brought these changes about using the kinds of political moves advocated for use under a system of LCMSG. Most changes were accomplished with social pressure, especially effective since the Queen was a friend, and with any legislative action held in abeyance, reserved to be used, but not actually used except as a last resort. While it is true that especially women came to feel constrained by this arrangement, it dealt with the ravages of the industrial revolution in a far healthier, more humane way than our present day Fascism. Under LCMSG, the gender role and other issues of modern times could be dealt with on a local, human to human basis, with the benefits of Victorian thinking regained.

The true causes and thinking of Victorianism are lost to our minds, ever since the rise of Fascism in the 1930's. We have to look hard to see them. One example is the old YMCAs which were originally conceived as a place for a young man to live in an environment of Christian fellowship, while getting established in the world. They were started without government aid, and without maximizing profit as their top priority. Another example of a last vestige of Victorian thinking is the Levittown housing developments started, with government encouragement, after World War II as a way for returning soldiers to purchase small, starter homes. That plan worked so well it is a wonder it hasn't been tried again.

Probably the most enduring example of this thinking comes from the movie, "It's a Wonderful Life" directed by Frank Capra. Think about the difference between the fictional towns of Bedford Falls and Pottersville. Bedford Falls, which had George Bailey, was full of stable, happy families living in little houses they owned. Pottersville was populated by renters living in rented rooms, with broken homes, prostitutes, liquor stores and taverns in abundance.

The only real difference between the two towns was the community mindedness of the town's leaders, and none of the difference was based on laws. In Bedford Falls, George Bailey heroically kept the Bailey Building and Loan going in the face of the evil banker Potter's opposition. Bailey Building and Loan was lending money to all the people in town to buy homes, build equity and establish good lives. In Pottersville, George Bailey had never been born (the overt message of the movie was how wonderful his life really was) and so banker Potter got to carry out all his greedy, community destroying schemes without opposition.

Coming from the hand of the immigrant Frank Capra, one can see that this movie is actually about the benefits of the kind of little freedoms Local Community Moral Self Government would give rise to, the kinds of freedom this section has been about, and that the fictional George Bailey brought to life. The proof of this interpretation of the movie is the last scene, which has probably puzzled many. The last scene is not a bell ringing on a Christmas tree, but is instead the Liberty Bell, being rung with wonderful abandon, celebrating the kind of freedom portrayed in the movie.

The kind of freedom portrayed in "It's a Wonderful Life", the kind of freedom practiced by the Victorians, is something that is largely lost to our memories, and that's a pity. It really is the third way in politics looked for by so many, and called for in "The Greening of America". Re-establishing a system of Local Community Moral Self Government would be moving toward that third way, calling us back to our roots, and to a system that has been proven to be a better system from the one we have today. It is far more thorough, efficient, and effective with dealing with the excesses of big business and the industrial revolution than our present two faced Fascist system. And it does so while avoiding the pitfalls of over-centralized government.

Some final points are in order. It is important to emphasize that LCMSG is merely an architecture of government, a certain way of arranging the powers of government, and does not dictate the content or policies of that government. Much as a building might house over time, different concerns ranging from a grocery store, to a church to a bank to a school to a car dealership or whatever, LCMSG could be the house for a wide range of different kinds of governing, from libertarian or anarchist to free marketeering to deeply socialist. What's more, since we would still be under our Constitution, we would continue to have the option of mandating, via constitutional amendment, that the entire nation conform to some governing philosophy or the other.

For instance, if over the course of time, the sentiment grew that we wanted to move more in the direction of centralized socialism, we could. A constitutional amendment could be passed that mandated a level of economic equality be guaranteed in every community. It would be wise, in the enactment of any such national mandate, that care be taken to ensure that such a mandate still be carried out at the local or state level, and the administration of something like economic equality not be handed over to some distant authority.

In that way, any new national mandate, be it socialistic, libertarian, or whatever, would be perceived by that multitude of local minds as just another speed bump, another obstacle or challenge, like those of providing clean water, sewage, a sound economy, and health care, etc., that "we" must meet and overcome together. In this way, the feedback loop of governance that produces good, morally uplifted citizens could be preserved, even as the nation moved together in that new direction. It would be good to keep the risk of such a move in mind however, because the original plan of the old Union of Soviet Socialist Republics was that each soviet would handle the administration of economic justice at the local level, but it soon devolved into the centralized, top down nightmare that ended up in the dust bin of history.

The final point in this chapter will also recall Marxism, and many other utopian schemes of government, such as Libertarianism or Anarchism. In most of these, there is the long term promise that if we establish those systems, they will work so well that over time the hearts and minds of the people will grow to the point that the state will fade away. The promise of the state fading away, and there not being a standing government has long been the hope of mankind, even as we have moved further and further from it. Local Community Moral Self Government is the only system, due to its incorporation of the feedback loop that affects the individual citizen, to actually raise the consciousness of the masses in such a way as to realistically promise such an outcome.

However, that glorious outcome is not being guaranteed, or even specifically promised here. Nonetheless, since LCMSG is founded with a focus on the consciousness of the individual, it is probably the only scheme of government likely to end there. All forms of Marxism and Fascism have reverted to elitism and have ended, and probably always will end, in some sort of authoritarianism. Libertarianism especially in its extreme forms, and Anarchism with their allowance of the dominance of the strong, will probably end in some sort of new feudalism. The fading of the state, and the end of standing government might never actually happen on this planet, but if it does, some form of Local Community Moral Self Government will be the vehicle it arrives in.

The morally uplifting feedback loop of LCMSG provides a way for individuals to grow in organic response to the challenges of the real world. If the state can fade away, this is how it will happen. It simply won't happen by some enlightened mindset being imposed from on high. That on-high-ness, is by definition government, and therefore doomed to fail. It is a built- in contradiction to expect the state to force the people to make the state fade away. People don't change that way, but it is a way to enslave them.

With all that said and promised, the next chapter will examine how we might conduct our revolution and actually re-establish Local Community Moral Self Government in America.

Footnotes:

[1.] *The Forgotten Man, A New History of the Great Depression*, Amity Shlaes, (HarperCollins Publishers, 10 East 53rd Street, New York, NY 10022, 2007) p.143

[2.] *The Outline of Sanity* "The Collected Works of G.K. Chesterton", Volume V, (Ignatius Press, San Francisco, 1987), p. 43

[3.] *Maverick Marine*, Hans Schmidt, (University of Kentucky Press, 1987), p. 231

[4.] *The Federalist Papers,* Clinton Rossiter- ed., (Signet Classic Printing, 275 Hudson St., NY, NY. 10014, 2003) p. 367

[5.] *Democracy in America* Alexis DeTocqueville 1835, (Penguin Books, London, England, 2003), p.805, 806

[6.] *The Death of Common Sense*, Phillip K. Howard, (Random House, NY, NY, 1994), p.173

[7.] *The Greening of America*, Charles A. Reich, (Crown Trade Paperbacks, 201 east 50th Street, New York, NY, 1970)

Chapter 6

How We Can Have a Revolution

"What Hath God Wrought?"

The first message sent by Samuel Morse to initiate the first telegraph service, 1844

"A man may die, nations may rise and fall, but an idea lives on."

John F. Kennedy, 1963

Apathy and Intimidation

The obvious conclusion from the preceding chapters is that we should do something to change our dysfunctional government. The happy fact is that the foundation of our system of government is still sound, even though a lot of shoddy, possibly even oppressive structure has been built on top of that foundation. Consequently, we, as Americans, have the great advantage that we can effect the needed changes. This can be established- not by completely demolishing our government and starting over from scratch, but rather by returning to the original foundation of the Constitution. So let us think about how we might reverse the blunders of the last 150 years and revive an honest use of our Constitution. We can regain for ourselves the blessings of liberty by returning the powers of economic, social, and moral self government to the people.

The first step to take in actually changing things is to admit that the reason it is so hard for us to do so is that Americans are deeply demoralized and intimidated, and that these two problems work together to keep us impotent. Demoralization has two meanings: for one, it can mean someone or some group is lacking in enthusiasm. The deeper meaning and- the one being applied here, is that someone or some group has lost the reason or motivation to be moral; they have become de-moralized.

With the almost total loss of the powers of self government that has been suffered by our communities, the normal person sees almost no reason to try to exert a moral influence on those around them. There just doesn't seem to be much purpose to doing so, since the moral decisions that we all have to live under are being made by those who are high above and far away.

This demoralization works hand in glove with the sense of intimidation thrown out by those high and distant authorities. Since there is little reason to be "moral', and since the mind of the flesh, to borrow a term from Christianity, is always present, calling us to a life of eat, drink, and be merry; or wine, women, and song; or sex, drugs, and rock and roll, or however the ancient mindset of debauchery is being packaged these days, we always have a tendency to stay apathetic about getting truly politically active. The payoff is that we can continue to indulge our petty desires.

This bias toward apathy is what causes us to so quickly abandon any effort to revive the country. We may sincerely want to do something, but there is always some imposing obstacle, legal precedent, adversarial party, or the anonymous "they" that won't let it happen. Since it is hard to see how our puny individual efforts can overcome such obstacles, we are easily tempted to abandon the effort without even starting. We tell ourselves such changes are impossible and will never happen. Thus we justify going back to our lives of self indulgent fear, at the least contenting ourselves with eating food and watching television.

"It will never happen" is the battle cry of the apathetic when anyone confronts them with a plan to change things in our country. One is reminded of two rats in separate cages in a lab; one rat is real smart, and the other rat is very ignorant. The bars of both cages are made of titanium, so the smart rat knows that he can never chew through them, and consequently never tries. The ignorant rat knows no such thing, so he spends his days gnawing on the bars of his cage, while the smart rat ridicules him with the taunt, "it will never happen." Then, of course, one morning the smart rat wakes up to find that the ignorant rat has succeeded at gnawing his way to freedom, and is gone. The lesson of this story being that the best way to intimidate folks is to cause them to think they know there is nothing to be done, that "it will never happen." That is exactly what has been done, and will continue to be done, to the people of this nation. Much as we might bemoan our impending doom, we have become convinced that nothing can be done to change the direction.

To get to the goals of this manifesto, we will first have to work our way past some powerful, intimidating arguments from the elitists. The first and most impressive of these emotional arguments is that if we decentralize both industry and government, we will risk losing all the material benefits of modern civilization. They want us to think we can't live well without their having all the power.

This is of course ridiculous. It is neither over-centralized corporate industry, nor over-centralized government that has brought about these modern benefits. Rather, it is the ongoing advance of science and the industrial revolution, which was going along just fine before all this centralization took place. After all, the telephone was invented in 1876, a full decade before the advent of corporate personhood. The locomotive and the telegraph were invented even earlier. Technological innovation- which extends to advances in agriculture, medicine, and transportation, enabling a much fuller diet, and healthier lives for us all, will continue even if we return corporate and governmental control to our local communities. We just want to be in a position to insist that the growth of technology benefits humanity, and doesn't instead cripple and enslave many of us.

In fact, there is a strong case to be made that the concentration of wealth has stifled the advance of the industrial revolution. Wealthy interests have sought to protect their sources of wealth by preventing technology from growing into areas that would threaten existing industries. They have not been above using the powers of over-centralized government to accomplish this when they needed, so both big government and big business don't necessarily bring us all that much progress. Decentralizing both certainly wouldn't imperil our civilization.

The second major argument the elites will throw at us to prevent a return to LCMSG is the one about the economy of scale. This argument, similar to the material gains argument, asserts that we gain so much by the economy of scale afforded by centralized government and business that any other approach would cause us to decline economically.

The problem with that thinking is that while it is irrefutable that an economy of scale, where huge numbers of products and services are standardized and thereby made much more efficiently, can be a great benefit, it happens only in theory. In the real world, corruption and greed can easily creep into any large, over-centralized institution, whether corporate or government, greatly reducing efficiency. What's more, to combat the corruption, over-centralized institutions are forced to resort to multiple layers of bureaucratic regulation, which also cuts deeply into efficiency. In the end, the advantages of an economy of scale promised by over-centralized business and government are largely theoretical and offset by the advantages offered by more accountable and flexible, de- centralized business and government.

The third major argument the elites will oppose us with will be much harder to resist, because it will probably never be spoken out loud. It is the one that most appeals to the dark, de-moralized side of our human nature. The social system we have in place today can rightly be termed a libertine socialism because citizens are allowed to live any way they choose, with socialism ensuring they won't get hurt. Lifestyles of promiscuity, drug use, sloth, obesity, drunkenness, abuse, etc., are allowed and even encouraged. Even if there is some kind of reckoning with the justice system for some, in the end, if one has made a wreck of their life, Uncle Sugar looms in the background, ready to accept the person as a disabled ward of the state, and put their life back together.

This libertine socialism, which separates the vital social aspects of authority and responsibility, appeals to the dark side of human nature like no system that ever existed. As DeTocqueville noted, this system treats all of us as children, and being able to behave as a lifelong child appeals to many of us. The big problem is, of course, that this separation of authority from responsibility, with citizens retaining authority over their lives to live any way they choose, and the government having the responsibility to keep those same lives from falling apart, is a social compact that cannot be sustained. Eventually, the party who has responsibility will begin and be able to assert more and more authority over the other party, leaving them eventually with no authority or responsibility. The inescapable truth is that authority and responsibility will always end up tied together.

Probably the only sure way to convince people that this libertine socialism is not a good thing (and it also appeals to those productive citizens who like not having to directly provide for or morally lift up the libertines) is to wait for the system to decline to the point where most of us are living in government dormitories. When we are drugged down, constantly monitored, provided with beds, meals, and little blue pajamas to live in, with our freedom reduced to being allowed to choose between hamburgers or spaghetti at the cafeteria, then we might realize it is a bad idea.

As it is, with this libertine socialism in place, guided by a calculating elitist materialism, that is where most of us "food eating breeders living in fly over country" are headed. What's more, given our desire to live irresponsible lives of self indulgence, that is where we deserve to go.

There is another way we might be convinced that this is the wrong path, but it involves our waking up, growing up, realizing we are on the edge of a cliff about to step into totalitarian despotism, turning around, and running the other way. One good definition of "Maturity" is regretting a mistake before one makes it. Whether or not we, as a people, are mature enough to recognize the abyss looming before us, and to step back from the precipice, is, unfortunately, an open question. Many of us are deeply concerned about the path this nation is on, but we are still hopelessly divided from each other, intimidated and apathetic. One side ignores its own shortcomings and shouts about the evils of big business. The other side is blind to its own defects and shouts about the evils of big government.

Technical Solutions

Assume for the moment that this unifying vision of American liberty (LCMSG) takes hold, and the great majority of the American people shakes off its demoralized, intimidated apathy and rises up to demand that it be followed. The technical means by which these changes could be accomplished are actually fairly simple. In the case of the First Amendment (and the issues of moral self government peripheral to it, like abortion, etc.) the solution would be for the Congress, guided by this vision of liberty, to exercise the check on the Court it has always had in the Constitution, contained in Article 3, Section 2, the second sentence of the second paragraph, which states:

"In all other cases before mentioned the supreme court shall have appellate jurisdiction, both as to law and fact, with such exceptions, and under such regulations, as the congress shall make."

All that has to happen is for Congress to make all First Amendment and other moral issues, when enacted by states or localities, an exception to the appellate jurisdiction of the Court, and we would immediately be returned to the original, honest use of the First Amendment, keeping any laws passed by the U.S. Congress subject to Supreme Court appeal. States would once again have to work out for themselves the issues of moral education, pornography, abortion, free speech, fighting and hate speech, and all the rest. If the U.S. Congress would attempt to make any law respecting the establishment of religion, or limiting speech or press, which would be a violation of the original intention of the First Amendment, a suit against such an act could still be appealed to the Supreme Court. So a proper use of the First Amendment would be restored, and the powers of moral self government returned to the states and localities.

In a similar manner, the issues around corporate personhood could be dealt with by a few fairly simple legal moves, once we assume the people were aroused and demanding the changes. First of all, the federal Congress, or even the Court, could reverse the doctrine of corporate personhood, taking corporations out from under the legal protection of the Fourteenth Amendment, and returning control of corporations to the states. That exception to the appellate jurisdiction of the Supreme Court might be useful here also.

At the same time, the idea that a corporation can conduct business in one state, and be regulated by the laws of another state would have to be annulled. At the same time, America would have to withdraw from, or at least demand changes to, some of the international trade agreements, such as NAFTA and the WTO.

The long term goal of these moves would be to return the control of corporations to states and local communities, but in the short term these changes would undoubtedly cause economic uncertainty and turmoil. Think about this though; the plants would still grow in the ground, machines and consumer goods would still be manufactured, planes, trains, ships and trucks could still move goods to market, and we could be pretty sure that the economy would continue to function. In the end, we would find that business continues to find a way to make a profit, although some corporations might not enjoy such enormous profits. More importantly, we would come to a place where the corporate beast has been brought to heel on the much shorter leash of community control. With that, the promise and force of the industrial revolution will be domesticated, and the people will benefit more from technological improvements, and the machines being used less to control the masses. Those would be some of the results of returning the powers of economic self government to the states and communities.

In both cases, that of moral self government and that of economic self government, the changes could come relatively quickly. If the masses were aroused and guided by this vision of revived American liberty, they could demand, through their elected officials, that the courts apply the newly accepted interpretation of the Constitution. Then, justices could either rule in that manner, leave by natural attrition to be replaced by justices holding to the vision of liberty, or be impeached for not faithfully applying the Constitution to the cases before the court. Impeachment of justices who insisted upon adjudicating American law based on something other than a clear reading of the Constitution would be both reasonable, and would hasten the advance of the agenda of liberty. To provide clear legal authority for us to impeach justices for this reason, we might have to enact a new amendment, but it is one that the vast majority of the people would support, because they assume it is already the case.

The solution in the case of the powers of social self government, Social Security and federal socialism in general, is more problematic but something we could accomplish. Since the time of FDR, and even a little before that, the actions of the federal government have been less and less in compliance with the limits placed on it by the Constitution. The worst aspect of our present situation in this regard is that, not only do many people want the federal government to carry out some of those functions; in some instances a strong case can be made that the feds should have some authority. For example, there has clearly arisen a need for some kind of federal authority regarding the environment, but just exactly what that authority should be, and how it should be limited, has never been determined, and it has not been enshrined as it ought, by constitutional amendment.

Consequently, the best way to proceed in returning the powers of social self government to local communities would be for the Congress, once again motivated by a populace demanding a return to liberty, to enact a continuing resolution. This resolution would list all the areas where actions of the federal government don't conform to the words of the Constitution, and then one by one, each issue would either be returned to the province of the states, or given proper authority as a federal power by ratification of a new constitutional amendment. This would be a many years long process, over the course of a number of congresses responding to the same continuing resolution, (even as, hopefully, the list of federal non compliance shrinks) and in the end, many of the responsibilities for maintaining the public good would have been returned to the states and localities, and those exercised by the federal government would have been delegated proper authority. We would then be passing on to future generations, with all these changes, a nation with free local community self government, and a functioning constitutional republic.

The issues of welfare and Social Security would be especially delicate, and take some real social growth to handle. The biggest problem with welfare is that many localities would early on realize that they might shirk any of these responsibilities, and lay them on other communities, thereby saving themselves a lot of money. As the national community became aware of this foot dragging and stinginess, it could be dealt with in a number of ways. Modern technology would give us the tools to selectively boycott the products coming out of the recalcitrant communities, tracking it down, for example, to a particular truckload of lumber from a particular mill. Then, the larger community would be able to make the stingy community aware that it is not alone, and that it should be a good member in the community of communities. If that didn't work, we could use the heavy hand of government to force compliance. Since we didn't really want to use that tool, and would only do so if the stingy community forced us, even after they had been forced to do their fair share, they would still be considered pariahs, and they would likely comply before it came to that point.

Social Security would require even more delicacy, because so many have paid into the system for decades, and have made plans based on having that money to sustain them. If we wind Social Security down, we must still ensure that all those who are dependent on the system are treated fairly. This could involve any number of options, from transitioning to state financing, lowering housing and hence nursing home costs through the little freedoms mentioned earlier, to shared housing and resorting back to families supporting the elderly. This is not to mention current proposals to ensure Social Security's solvency, such as raising the age of eligibility, or means testing benefits. While fairness to the elderly is a strong argument, it must always be balanced with fairness to the young, who are paying much more, as a percentage of their earnings, into the system than the current elderly did, and yet can expect much less to nothing out of it when their time comes.

These changes will be very difficult. So much of the difficulty is due to the fact that socialism in general, and Social Security in particular are addictions, and all addictions seem, to the addict, to be impossible to break. To make matters worse, since this is an addiction of our entire society, those who might be hurt by the process of ending the addiction will be inclined to try to kick the problem down the road, so that someone later will have to deal with an even bigger problem.

The current recipients will see themselves as victims, and in some ways they inevitably will be. Social Security is a large Ponzi scheme, and the reason Ponzi schemes are illegal is that they always leave many victims in their wake. So it will take our honesty, courage, wisdom, and compassion to break this addiction, but break it we must. This socialism we have inherited, Social Security in particular, is an addictive, corrosive social poison that will continue to eat away at our families, our culture and our collective souls until it is ended.

Obstacles in Communication

All of these changes actually coming about are based on the assumption that the masses become properly enlightened about the blessings of liberty, and aroused to demand its return. Needless to say, that's a pretty big assumption. As a matter of fact, rousing the people to get even one of these changes would probably be well nigh impossible. Even more challenging, all of the changes have to be made, with the entire bundle of self governing powers returned to local communities, for the positive dynamics proposed here to get real traction.

It has been said that the only thing a tyrant fears is an aroused populace. However, achieving and maintaining that level of political arousal over the course of many years is impossible to conceive of in our present cultural environment. Frankly, our society is dominated in the areas of government, education, and media by a fascist oligarchy that doesn't want any of these changes to happen. The supposedly diverse media, with both conservative and liberal outlets, is far from the free marketplace of ideas that we could hope for. In fact, the cable and radio talk shows function more to keep the minds of the people solidly entrenched in one of two channels, than as vehicles for free and honest dialogue intent to find solutions to our problems.

In spite of the oligarchy's dominance of the means of communication, it might be possible to get the people engaged or mad enough, to get some one thing changed. That would probably be the end of the changes, and as noted earlier, the restoration of liberty requires at least three major changes be made. Consequently, in order to have a realistic chance of succeeding with this agenda, we must come up with a single, short term strategic goal. It must be something that would allow us to break the hold the oligarchy has on the means of communication, and thereby enable us to pursue the rest of the agenda.

At this point it will be instructive to look at the history of the media in this country. In a process that was taking place at the same time as the other historical processes examined in this book, (the experience of African-Americans, the growth of corporate power after the advent of corporate personhood, the growth of federal power under FDR socialism, and the 180 degree twisting of the First Amendment) the mass media came under the control of corporations.

As a short aside, with all these concurrent streams of action going on over decades and centuries, it is easy to see why our complex nation, with its intertwined problems, is so intimidating, and hard to grasp. Our problems are very complex, requiring complex solutions that don't lend themselves to the sound bite demagoguery so prevalent today.

Now we will look at how the changes happened to the mass media, why they were so contrary to the spirit of American liberty, and how a means of reversing that process offers us that one issue with which we might restore the entire fabric of liberty. Things started out quite well with the federal government prohibited from controlling the press in any way, so that a nearly unlimited number of voices could be heard. Circa 1835, Alexis DeTocqueville noted,

"In the United States printers need no licenses, and newspapers no stamps or registrations; moreover, the system of giving securities is unknown.

For these reasons it is a simple and easy matter to start a paper; a few subscribers are enough to cover expenses, so the number of periodical or semi-periodical productions in the United States surpasses all belief." [1]

That all started to change with the invention of the telegraph. After Samuel Morris sent his famous question of "What Hath God Wrought?" on the first telegraph message, the nature of the media started to lend itself to centralization. Some of the richer newspapers could afford to lay telegraph lines from Washington, D.C. to places like New York City, where they could publish the latest happenings in the halls of Congress days before the competition was able. Since the public preferred publications with the latest news, the big papers saw circulation swell, and then they were in a position to charge more to firms advertising on their pages, so much so that they could charge even less for the papers sold on the streets, and drive competing newspapers into bankruptcy. This was the beginning of the penny newspapers, and the number of newspapers (and the diversity of voices) began to decline markedly. The media was becoming centralized.

The process of centralization continued slowly throughout the 1800's, with the consolidation of wire services (fewer actual voices) to supply telegraphed news to the smaller papers so they could remain competitive, and the advent of national newspaper chains, like the Hearst papers. Centralization of the media then greatly accelerated with the coming of radio, followed by television in the early 1900's. Since both these formats have limited bandwidth available, not everyone can start a station. They must first get government approval to operate on a particular frequency. The Federal Communications Commission and the Fairness Doctrine were rear guard efforts to ensure that the electronic media contained a "free marketplace of ideas", without which it was feared the power of the new technology could jeopardize our entire way of life. However, the efforts to create said free marketplace of ideas have largely failed.

By the 1990's, Ben Baghdikian could point out in his book, "Media Monopoly" that the 27 (or fewer) people, enough to fill a good sized dinner party, with the right corporate positions would be able to control one hundred percent of the electronic media in this country, and almost all of the print media. Media ownership has become even more concentrated since that time. What's more, all of them share some important interests. They are all rich, and they are all well connected politically. Therefore, it is unlikely that they would help to bring about any truly revolutionary change. Once again, there might not be a conspiracy afoot here, but it sure looks like one to those on the outside. [2]

The bigger point is that when the founders prohibited the government from controlling the press, they thought that they were ensuring that a free and honest dialogue would always take place. They did not foresee the cultural changes that the growth of technology might bring, and they certainly could not have foreseen that the interests of wealth could come to exercise a form of media control just as threatening to liberty as any governmental censorship. What's more, with the kind of informal conspiracy of the real Fascism that has been discussed, we can see that this corporate monopoly on the media might be serving the goals of some despotic agenda just as surely as if official government censorship were allowed.

Revolution

Let's look at one more aside before the single unifying concept is proposed. The word "revolution" is now going to be discussed. What we need, and what is called for here is a revolution, which is not the same as a call for violence. In truth, times of true revolution are usually not violent, and times of great violence are rarely revolutionary. To clear this point up, let's consider the definition of revolution that will be used here.

Revolution: To consider the long sweep of history, whether local, state, national, or global; figure out what we did wrong and stop doing it; figure out what we did right, do more of it, and then carry on.

This definition of revolution is centered on communication as the means of revolution. Consider the famous "revolutions" of past and current times. If a time of great upheaval and violence does not result in a time of honest, open dialogue, then that "revolution" turns out to be a failure, as were the French and Russian revolutions. On the other hand, if that time of honest and open communication can be achieved through non violent means, then that is a time of great revolution. For example, the era in America when non property owners gained the right to vote, the women's suffrage movement, and the civil rights movement were all relatively non violent, and yet brought great revolutionary changes through open dialogue creating deeper mutual understanding.

Consider this passage, written by John Adams in a letter to Thomas Jefferson dated 8-24-1815. "What do we mean by the revolution? The war? That was no part of the revolution, it was only an effect and consequence of it. The revolution was in the hearts and minds of the people, and this was effected from 1760 to 1775, in the course of fifteen years, before a drop of blood was shed at Lexington".

On the international scene, Bishop Desmond Tutu and the "Truth Commissions" in South Africa have brought about many beneficial changes by focusing on a non-violent, communications based revolutionary process. As a matter of fact, since real progress in human affairs is based upon such open and honest communication, and times of violence usually prevent that kind of dialogue, times of violence are usually anti-revolutionary.

Open Media

With all that said, we now look at that single unifying concept which might be the first step in reviving Local Community Moral Self Government. Simply stated, this proposal calls for the establishment, through the use of electronic media of a national public forum, a truly free market place of ideas. There are a lot of details to fill in, and obvious objections to meet, but the basic parameters would call for each person to be able to address the nation on live, unedited broadcast television and radio, and for the citizenry as a whole to decide whether or not any particular person gets more time on the live broadcast forum. No laws would be passed by this public forum, but the people would have a real voice in public opinion, and some real influence in the direction public opinion moves.

This proposal for a nationwide public forum, which will be referred to as the Open Media, would first of all, be established by enactment of an amendment to the Constitution. The way that this proposal strategically fits into and enables the larger agenda of restoring American liberty is that it is a single concept which can focus the energies of all lovers of liberty. Once enacted, such a forum would enable the lovers of liberty to have a fighting chance to continue to arouse public opinion, in spite of the opposition of the rich and powerful. The multi-faceted, multi-years liberty agenda might actually be accomplished.

To better understand the Open Media, let's consider three major aspects of the proposal. First, we will look at the details of how such a forum might work, and why it is necessarily so different from the so called "forums" on the media and internet of today. Second, we will need to consider why establishing the Open Media by constitutional amendment is appropriate, and how such a move is in concert with the thinking of the founders of our republic. Finally, it will be good to envision how many benefits a forum of this type could bring to this and any nation, over and above the benefit of enabling us to make solid moves in the agenda of restoring liberty.

Let's look at how the Open Media would operate. Keep in mind that while it will seem like this outline is perhaps too specific, most of the guidelines offered here have been well thought out. While they could stand some modification, most are necessary if the organic nature of an Open Media is to thrive.

Each citizen would be given two minutes on live, unedited television and radio to address their fellow citizens. Then every citizen would be given one vote to determine if that person gets more time later on the same live forum. Since the numbers don't work to allow everyone two minutes on a nationwide forum, the Open Media would be based on local, state, and national forums. A person would first get a chance to be on a local forum, live and unedited, for two minutes. In the local area, every citizen would get one vote of feedback, either through the phone system or a web site. That vote would determine which of the speakers received more time on the forum, a week or so later. It would be a simple majority vote, and if the speaker lost, he or she would have to go back to the end of the line. That queue would be designed to take approximately two years to have the opportunity to return. In this way every opportunity would be seen as precious.

If the speaker won the vote, he or she would get more time on the live, unedited forum, and each time on the forum, the citizenry as a whole would be allowed to participate in a feedback vote, to decide whether or not to bring that person back into the forum. The top vote getters in each locality would be given time on a statewide live unedited forum, where they could address a larger audience of citizens. Once again they would receive a feedback vote by the audience. That statewide feedback vote would determine which participants received more time on the statewide forum, and the top vote getters in each state would be eligible to participate on a nationwide live unedited forum.

On the national forum, the same rules would apply, in that each participant would get two minutes to begin, and the citizenry as a whole would get to vote to determine who gets more time on the forum. Since there wouldn't be a worldwide forum, top vote getters wouldn't go to a higher level, but they would continue to be heard until the people no longer voted to hear from them, or whatever they were advocating was accomplished, either through legislative action or social change, and they no longer wished to continue.

That is the basic idea of the Open Media, with a few refinements to be added now, and later in the discussion as certain topics come up. The first point is to emphasize that no laws would be passed on this forum, so that it would not be an instantaneous electronic democracy. All legislative process would remain as it is today, but the Open Media would change the way that public opinion is formed and heard.

Since some ideas would be much more important and timely than others, it would be wise to have a way of granting more than just the basic two minutes to those who win the feedback vote on any forum. For example, if on the local level, a first round participant won with a vote of ten thousand to nine thousand five hundred, it would be obvious that the public was very interested, so they would warrant a return to the forum sooner than someone who won the first round by a vote of five to one. Similarly, someone who won the feedback vote by a large margin of say five thousand to ten would warrant more time than someone who barely won a majority. Therefore, some kind of sliding scale based on numbers of people voting in the feedback vote, and margin of victory, would determine how soon one returned to the forum, and how long one was permitted to speak. At the same time, there would have to be a minimum amount of time, and return date that every winner, no matter how small the margin, would be guaranteed.

Another important aspect of the Open Media would be that participants would not only not be edited or pre-screened. Additionally, like members of Congress speaking on the floor of the legislature, participants on the Open Media would be exempt from slander and libel laws while they spoke on the forum. This is the only way to ensure that there would be a full and honest discussion of the issues. The Constitution grants that exemption to Congress and it gets to the point of why it is so appropriate that the Open Media be established by constitutional amendment.

Also, the Open Media would have to frankly commandeer time from the broadcast outlets, at least in the beginning. Over time we could anticipate some sort of direct satellite broadcast channel, dedicated to the public forum(s). The original amendment would call for a minimum amount of time per week for the Open Media, with the ability to expand built in from the first. If we decided to go below the minimum, to do away with the Open Media, that action would take a separate constitutional amendment.

Some might object that the cost would be prohibitive. In this age of information, when the most common problem is being inundated with worthless, manipulative information, would the cost of giving amplification to the free voice of the people really be a problem?

Also over time, the most used form of mass media might change, so a wisely written amendment would take that into account, mandating that whatever the most accessible format of communication available, some of it be reserved for use by the Open Media.

This commandeering of broadcast time would fit well with the long held principle, from the U.S. Supreme Court, that the airwaves are public property, and that therefore the broadcasters have a civic duty to serve the public good. Hosting a true public forum is definitely a public good, and could be seen as the fulfillment of that civic duty.

The Open Media would be fitting and appropriate for an even deeper reason. From the earliest days of the republic, third class mail, intended to transport books and periodicals has been subsidized, because it was reasoned that a democratic republic needed informed and educated citizens if it was to function properly. Even though third class mail has today come to be mostly used by commercial junk mail, the original principle of using government funds to ensure that the masses are informed and educated is still valid. The Open Media would be a very appropriate way to fulfill that vital founding mandate in our high tech world.

With the dynamic of Open Media up and growing, it could be anticipated that some would begin to use their time on the forum to sing, dance, show artwork, show videos, or whatever. That would be fine, as we would want to encourage everyone to be as fully expressive and free as possible. Nonetheless, to ensure that the Open Media won't cater to the questionable desires of those who wish to remain anonymous, with all the potential for mischief that implies, we would be wise to stipulate that every one must have their name, face, and home town presented to the public for the first and last five seconds of their presentation. Everything else, all of the remaining allotted time could be used however the person wished.

This might seem like a rather arbitrary and overly detailed stipulation, but it serves to bring up the larger point that the idea here is to try to get an organic, living kind of dialogue going, and then give the power of electronic amplification to that free and honest voice of the people. That is why the idea is to make sure that everyone gets a chance to speak freely and has an equal say about who gets more time. Yet there is a sense of accountability and responsibility put on the participants, so that this tool of self government is put to serious and sober use by the people. That is why we should arrange things so that a person gets that first chance at the local level only every two years. Everyone who is on the free forum is seen openly, and will therefore be accountable to their local community. .

It must be admitted that the specific form and rules for the Open Media can and likely will be improved upon, especially as people put their minds to the task. One thing we can all agree upon is that we don't currently have that open, free marketplace of ideas.

The much touted town hall meetings held by elected officials, political candidates, and media personalities are a far cry from a free market place of ideas. Those entering the hall are usually pre-screened for the correct political opinions before they enter, and those allowed to ask a question are pre-screened yet again. Then, if some sort of "subversive" voice does get heard, the "moderator" handles it with a high handed, crafty technique that evades any kind of real dialogue.

The forums and chat boards on the internet are scarcely much better. First of all, in order to participate, one must have access to a computer, and be able to express ideas in writing. That eliminates a lot of people who might have good ideas. Then, there is no valid way of determining who is winning one of these internet debates, which is probably why so many of them become name calling contests. Also, most allow participants to remain anonymous which also tends to diminish the truthfulness and accountability of the debates.

Talk radio is more of the same, only worse. It is almost always anonymous, and there is no way of determining what the audience thinks about the debate. Add to that the egos, and commercial motivations of the talk show hosts, and their ability to use the entire range of cheap rhetorical and highhanded talk show tricks, and the dialogue rarely qualifies as a free and open marketplace of ideas. Generally, radio and television talk show hosts are merely mind herders, serving to keep the minds of the listeners firmly entrenched on one side or the other of the fascist oligarchy.

Contrast the sorry state of public dialogue today with what could happen with the Open Media up and running. Restoring LCMSG is probably impossible without first establishing the Open Media, but restoring LCMSG would not be the only benefit of establishing an Open Media. Systematically amplifying the free voice of the people will be revolutionary in its own right, because the people can express and seek the whole truth, unencumbered by any corporate or government elites. The big boys simply wouldn't be able to stop a good idea from being heard, over and over again. Individuals could express their whole thought, and find what fellow citizens think in an open, free and honest process.

What's more, the Open Media provides means of accountability to individuals and communities. It would be a way for people to keep all levels of government, local, state, and national, more honest and uncorrupt. It would also provide the same tools for dealing with corrupt, abusive, or polluting corporations. With an Open Media it wouldn't be so easy to push the little guy around.

A related aspect of the Open Media is that it would be a means for the downtrodden and oppressed to gain a measure of justice. This would not only apply to the attaining of justice in regards to current issues, but an Open Media would be a way for otherwise ignored and powerless voices to be heard in the extremely diverse nation we would be with LCMSG. The laudable goal of the true liberal, defense of the weak, would be more assured and enabled with free and open public forums, at the local, state, and national level, than it is with any institution in place today. In this way, the entire strategy of LCMSG, with the necessary first step of an Open Media, meets the demands of the most idealistic of liberals.

The electronic mass media hasn't been used to amplify the free voice of the people, nor have the masses stepped forward and demanded that such a thing happen. It might be a cliché, but consider what the founders, men like Jefferson and Adams, would do if they could be transported to our time, and given the power to change some aspect of our society. If the revolutionary spirit of 1776 were to be resurrected, and they could see the way that the national dialogue has become dominated by big money interests, they would almost undoubtedly call for some kind of public forum as a first step in reversing the decline. They could certainly draw from history of their time to see how important some kind of free and open public forum is for a free republic to flourish.

With all that said, it has to be admitted that establishing an Open Media might not be the best or only strategy to pursue. Some of those who come to agree with this vision of liberty, might object that instead of a years long process, we could speed things up, and use the constitutional mechanism of calling a national convention for the purpose of enacting new amendments (Article 5). While such a move would be perfectly constitutional, in this corrupt time such a convention would surely fall under the control of the ruling fascists, and earn all the credibility of the latest Democratic or Republican Party conventions.

The better way of having such a convention would be in public, over the course of years, based on a truly open and meaningful discussion among all the people; in other words, establishing an Open Media. What's more, after an Open Media was established, and the public returned to being in charge of public opinion, we might come to a point in time where it would be a good idea to call a convention for proposing a bunch of amendments all at once. Either way, establishing an Open Media would be the best, first step.

Nonetheless, there might be some other ways to advance this agenda of liberty. As an instructive aside, let's look at how the most recent revolution in America, the Civil Rights movement, actually unfolded. In the book, "An American Insurrection, The Battle of Oxford, Mississippi, 1962" by William Doyle, the episode of James Meredith gaining entrance to the University of Mississippi reveals much about that time.

James Meredith, acting as an individual, unaffiliated with the NAACP, or Dr. Martin Luther King, Jr., won admission to the University as its first African-American student. In doing so, he revealed something of the Civil Rights movement that has wide application to our situation today.

After the end of World War II, African-Americans came home, after helping to win a war against racism, to resume their place in a racist society. This was widely seen as intolerable, and consequently many in the African-American community began to do whatever they could to change the situation. There was a general agitation, a time when everyone was agitating as best they could, most doing the things they knew to be right, so when someone rose as a leader, they recognized him, and the critical mass had grown that was able to change things.

Into this scenario stepped people like Rosa Parks, Martin Luther King, and James Meredith. Some had success, but most didn't. But as that level of general unrest was alive and growing, when Martin Luther King arose with the idea of non violent civil disobedience, it resonated with the whole community, and most other activists rushed to join in what looked like a winning formula. Their success is our history.

The lesson for us today is for each of us to try to move society in the best way she or he can. If each of us concerned for the fate of the nation catches this vision of liberty, and becomes active in pushing for reform, a critical mass of unrest will grow again. When a winning strategy appears, we will be in a position to get behind it, together. So whatever that winning strategy might prove to be, we will come together behind it, in a timely manner, if we are all, individually and collectively, doing the things we know to be right in seeking to re-establish our liberty.

What's more, if that first winning strategy proves to be establishing an Open Media, that general unrest would find more focused expression and more quickly produce a coherent, unifying agenda. Establishing an Open Media would be a way to initiate one of those upward spirals of government, with free and open dialogue bringing about positive changes, which inspires even more free and open dialogue. Not only will it give us the tools to achieve the larger goal of LCMSG, but by itself, the Open Media provides tools for reaching the most idealistic and liberal minded goals, goals to be fought for in every generation. To put it in the terms of formal philosophy, an Open Media is not only a necessary cause for a non-violent revolution, it may also be a sufficient cause.

While we continue the struggle for justice, let's keep our eye on the vision of liberty that we can now achieve. It will take years, if not decades, to regain what has been lost, and to do liberty better than ever, but it can be done. We will know when we have gone far enough, when we have consolidated that critical number of powers at the local level, and the citizenry has begun to accept the responsibilities of society. We will know it by the general rise in involvement and public awareness, and by a concurrent decline in crime and incivility. We will know we have gone far enough when the political concerns on the minds of the people are almost all centered on the local town hall and school boards. When the normal mode of involvement is to go down to the local meeting with a couple of friends to make sure things don't get out of hand. Then we will have gotten back to the home we never really lived in yet, that land dedicated to true liberty and justice for all, a free and self governing America.

Think about what a fully functioning nation with LCMSG and a working Open Media would look like. The intelligentsia, the natural elite that all societies have, would not be ruling over us like little gods. They would instead be intertwined with the masses, rubbing shoulders with the poor, working, and middle classes. As such, they would be moral and cultural leaders in our communities, and they would also remain connected with the advancing thinking of the rest of the country and world.

The Open Media would provide a means for us to oppose corruption. With the open, unstoppable communication it would enable, the people in general, and the intelligentsia in particular would have a way of rallying the masses to enforce justice, keep would be oppressors at bay, and make sure the industrial revolution stays domesticated. Think of all the legitimate powers that the federal government is supposed to use to keep local and state governments in check. With the Open Media, we would have a way to insist that it uses those powers correctly, and thus we could move into the era of Local Community Moral Self Government with a great deal of confidence.

This is not just a bunch of theory. While an electronically amplified public forum has never been established, history does provide a few examples of public forums in action, and they have always proven to be a boon to mankind.

The most prominent of these historical public forums was in the ancient city state of Athens, Greece. Athens at the time, was involved in a long struggle with Sparta, and due to that war, times were perilous. To maintain public confidence and good order, the leader of Athens, a man named Pericles, opened up the deliberations of government to all free males. (Still not slaves or women, but better than what had gone before.) This radical move worked very well, as Athens survived the wars. What's more important, the flowering of thought that the open public forum ignited, with names like Socrates, Plato, and Aristotle involved, has benefited the world for eons. That time is now known as "The Golden Age of Pericles".

Athens is not the only example. At the time of the Renaissance in Europe, the flowering of art, music, and thought produced works that still inspire and move us today. The early days of America, with things like the New England town meeting, wherein every voice got heard, and the people reasoned together in a free and open way, produced thinking that continues to guide us. When we look at the long sweep of history, those rare and precious moments when people were free, or at least much more free than normal to speak and reason together openly, have always been the basis for some kind of golden age, or cultural awakening.

To take an even longer look at the human past, that same phenomenon of free and open reasoning being at the basis of lasting societies, is probably universally true. The basic pattern of human development has been for tribes of nomads, hunter gatherers, etc. to occupy some land area. The tribal groups compete with each other for land and resources, so there is almost endless fighting. From Africa to the Americas to Europe and Asia, the tribal groups that sustained were the ones that brought the masses of the people into the decisions of the tribe. Some tribes might have a dominant strongman, and under him conquer for a season, but over time the people would turn away, and that tribe would lose power. For the most part, the tribes and small republics that brought the masses of the people into the decision making process were the ones that retained the confidence of the people, and sustained over time.

The Rise and Fall of Civilizations

Going beyond forums, let's look at entire societies. The more successful tribes would settle into small local republics and/or, city states like the ones that covered Greece in ancient times. Then, as these city states warred with each other, and with outside enemies, some one, or group of them would come to dominate, and an empire would be formed. Since it is difficult and rare to hold a republic together over a large empire, the empire would become despotic and corrupt, and sow the seeds for its eventual demise. Then, after the fall of the civilized empire, with no one mourning the passing of its foul, corrupt corpse, the people would fall into barbarism, start to reform into small nomadic or hunter gatherer tribes, and the process of building civilization would start all over again.

Just a cursory glance around at familiar history will confirm this version of human development. Rome is the latest of the ancient empires to collapse, and it was certainly a foul, corrupt corpse when it did. It had grown from the Etruscans, and the small republic of Rome. Over time, their successes led to such wealth that the republic fell. That changed the life of the people, allowed the rich to dominate the land, and sowed the seeds of their own destruction.

The pattern of tribes to small republics to large governments to empire to collapse and back to barbarism and tribalism has happened many times, long back into the mists of pre history. Look at the record of Sargon the Great, the history of places like Nineveh and Babylon and so forth. In America, we can see distinct stages from the recent history of the Original Nations. The Iroquois were at the stage of having a form of republic that was so effective that other tribes desired to join them. They were at a very good stage, and had not yet entered the stage of empire and decline.

The Aztecs, on the other hand, had already become so strong that they were dominating and oppressing their neighbors. Things were bad enough that when the Spaniards came on the scene, the neighboring tribes were eager to join them in overthrowing the Aztecs. In the American west, some tribes were still in the nomadic hunter gatherer stage while others, like the Navajo and Hopi, were starting into the city state stage.

In all the Original American tribes, the men were noted as great warriors. This is understandable because, since they were at the tribal or city state stage of development, every one had to do their part to help the tribe survive. This included fighting in wars. This has to be contrasted with the European mode at the time, where the nobles didn't really want the peasants to know how to fight. War for them, before the era of total war, was limited to gentlemen and professionals.

Let's focus on the strong warriors, the involved citizens of the tribes and small republics of the Original Americans. That type of person, a person with what has been termed "republican virtues" is largely the point of this manifesto. It has long been noted by social and political thinkers that small republics produce the republican virtues, aroused and involved citizens who are capable of self government.

The problem is that while these small republics produce great citizens, they also produce never ending wars with their neighbors. So the tendency is to go for the larger nation, accepting a decline in citizenship in the interest of peace. The problem becomes that a national government can develop a vested interest in never ending war, a kind of military industrial complex, and so we end up with a society with weak citizens and never ending war anyway.

The American Experiment

The obvious solution is to find a way to fit small republics into a larger, federated national structure. That is not an easy thing to do without risking despotism. The essence of the American experiment was to establish just such a system, one that preserved the republican virtues generated by Local Community Moral Self Government, and yet had the advantages; no small wars, a continental economy, free trade, a common defense, etc. of a national government. In other words, America was to be an incubator of republican virtues in the hearts and minds of the people, under a federated system of checks and balances. Needless to say, the outcome of the experiment is still in doubt.

After the Constitution was written, and before it was ratified, a debate over ratification raged throughout the nation, and a lot of that debate has been preserved in writing of what are called “The Federalist Papers” and “The Anti Federalist Papers.” Some of the thinking and warnings of the anti –federalists are very apropos to this discussion, so we will look at some of them.

The following was printed in “The New York Journal” October 18, 1787, under the pen name of “Brutus”.

“If respect is to be paid to the opinion of the greatest and wisest men who have ever thought or wrote on the science of government, we shall be constrained to conclude, that a free republic cannot succeed over a country of such immense extent, containing such a number of inhabitants, and these increasing in such rapid progression as that of the whole United States. Among the many illustrious authorities which might be produced to this point, I shall content myself with quoting only two. The one is the Baron de Montesquieu, “Spirit of Laws”. Chap. xvi. Vol.1 (book VIII) ‘It is natural to a republic to have only a small territory, otherwise it cannot long subsist. In a large republic there are men of larger fortunes, and consequently of less moderation; there are trusts too great to be placed in any single subject; he has interest of his own; he soon begins to think that he may be happy, great and glorious, by oppressing his fellow citizens; and that he may raise himself to grandeur on the ruins of his country.” [3]

The Pennsylvania convention ratified the Constitution on December 12, 1787. Twenty-one of those delegates voting against ratification issued a dissenting report December 18, 1787, telling why they objected, echoing "Brutus".

"We dissent, first, because it is the opinion of the most celebrated writers on government, and confirmed by uniform experience, that a very extensive territory cannot be governed on the principles of freedom, otherwise than by confederation of republics, possessing all the powers of internal government; but united in the management of their general, and foreign concerns…"

"We dissent, secondly, because the powers vested in Congress by this constitution, must necessarily annihilate and absorb the legislative, executive, and judicial powers of the several states, and produce from their ruins one consolidated government, which from the nature of things will be an iron handed despotism, as nothing short of the supremacy of despotic sway could connect and govern these United States under one government." [4]

"Brutus" again, from October 18, 1787, "This government is to possess absolute and uncontrollable power, legislative, executive, and judicial, with respect to every object to which it extends, for by the last clause of section 8th, article 1st, it is declared 'that the Congress shall have power to make all laws which shall be necessary and proper for carrying into execution the foregoing powers, and all other powers vested by this constitution, in the government of the United States, or in any department or office thereof.' And by the 6th article, it is declared 'that this constitution, and the laws of the United States, which shall be made in pursuance thereof, and the treaties made, or which shall be made, under the authority of the United States, shall be the supreme law of the land, and the judges in every state shall be bound thereby, any thing in the constitution, or law of any state to the contrary notwithstanding.' It appears from these articles that there is no need of any intervention of the state governments, between the Congress and the people, to execute any one power vested in the general government, and that the constitutions and laws of every state are nullified and declared void, so far as they are or shall be inconsistent with this constitution, or the laws made in pursuance of it, or with treaties made under the authority of the United States." [5]

This is why the first Congress passed, and the states ratified, the Tenth Amendment, so that some kind of limit existed on the federal government. That is why Jefferson warned of how corrupt the federal government could be if it ever got out of constitutional restraints, and a situation of one federal law applying to the entire nation obtained. And that is why Franklin Roosevelt's actions were such a deep betrayal of the American cause.

Let's return to the thinking of the Anti-Federalists, once again the Pennsylvania minority dissent. "The judicial powers vested in Congress are also so various and extensive, that by legal ingenuity they may be extended to every case, and thus absorb the state judiciaries, and when we consider the decisive influence that a general judiciary would have over the civil polity of the several states, we do not hesitate to pronounce that this power, unaided by the legislative, would effect a consolidation of the states under one government." [6]

"Brutus" echoed that sentiment, January 31, 1788,"This power in the judicial will enable them to mould the government, into almost any shape they please..." [7]

"The Federal Farmer" wrote on October 8 and 9, 1787, "And therefore, unless the people shall make some great exertions to restore to the state governments their powers in matters of internal police; as the powers to lay and collect, exclusively, internal taxes, to govern the militia, and to hold the decisions of their own judicial courts upon their own laws final, the balance cannot possibly continue long; but the state government must be annihilated, or continue to exist for no purpose." [8]

The great concern of these learned leaders was laid out earlier, "In a large republic there are men of larger fortunes, and consequently of less moderation; there are trusts too great to be placed in any single subject; he has interest of his own; he soon begins to think that he may be happy, great and glorious, by oppressing his fellow citizens; and that he may raise himself to grandeur on the ruins of his country."

Or as "Brutus" put it elsewhere in the same letter, "Besides, it is a truth confirmed by the unerring experience of ages, that every man, and every body of men, invested with power, are ever disposed to increase it, and to acquire a superiority over every thing that stands in their way." [9]

"In so extensive a republic, the great officers of government would soon become above the control of the people, and abuse their power to the purpose of aggrandizing themselves, and oppressing them." [10]

"Centinal" wrote in #1, October 5, 1787, "If it were not for the stability and attachment which time and habit give to forms of government, it would be in the power of the enlightened and aspiring few, if they should combine, at any time to destroy the best establishments, and even make the people the instruments of their own subjugation." [11]

Sound familiar to what has happened to us? Listen to the words of Melancton Smith, spoken at the convention to ratify the Constitution in New York, June 23, 1788, "If this government becomes oppressive, it will be by degrees: It will aim at its end by disseminating sentiments of government opposite to republicanism; and proceed from step to step in depriving the people of a share in the government." [12]

Once again, these words seem deeply prophetic when we consider how things have gone in this nation. A couple more passages from "The Anti-Federalist Papers" are in order. "The Federalist Farmer" wrote, October 8 and 9, 1787, "It must be granted, that if men hastily and blindly adopt a system of government, they will as hastily and as blindly be led to alter or abolish it; and changes must ensue, one after another, till the peaceable and better part of the community will grow weary with changes, tumults and disorders, and be disposed to accept any government, however despotic, that shall promise stability and firmness." [13]

Once again, the idea that there are upward and downward spirals in government is not a new one.

On January 3, 1788, "Cato" wrote, "Montesquieu observes that 'the course of government is attended with an insensible descent to evil, and there is no re-ascending to good without very great efforts.'". [14]

Given the warring nature of small republics on their own, and the despotic nature of centralized governments, LCMSG is probably the natural end of human government on this earth. It is undoubtedly worth our making the "great effort" to revive our original form of government.

Even if we fail, this idea of Local Community Moral Self Government, held together with checks and balances in a larger national federated system will be tried again (and again and again) until we humans get it right. As President John Kennedy said "A man may die, nations may rise and fall, but an idea lives on." [15]

So even if our experiment in sustainable government fails, it will have helped advance human wisdom. It will not be the last time that humanity will attempt to find that healthy balance between free small republics and peaceful larger nations. When seen in that long light of history, America is not, as many have said, the last best hope of humanity, rather it is the latest best hope. If we don't get it right, and we, along with the rest of humanity, revert to barbarism after a lengthy interlude in the wonderful land of totalitarian despotism, we will eventually get back up on our hind feet, and start all over again. But in the end, one way or another, one time or another, the only possible end of human government, the only way it can ever be stable and sustainable, will be with some form of Local Community Moral Self Government in a federated national or even global structure.

So to sum up the agenda here, this manifesto is calling for a re-founding of this nation on its original principles, not merely rebuilding things on little understood ideas and empty slogans from the past. This movement toward Local Community Moral Self Government is definitely NOT about slavishly holding to the dead words of some dead white men, but is instead impelled by the realization that the government that was composed from 1776 to 1787 in the United States of America frames and defines a form of government that, in a way almost unique on this planet, empowers the people to find a way to true liberty and justice for all.

This book has presented a vision of a feasible and attainable alternative to the Fascist trap set before us. It is a vision that government of, by, and for the people might live, and not perish. From establishing Local Community Moral Self Government to using the Open Media to do so, these are specific proposals and plans of action that embody the kind of eternal themes that President Kennedy was referring to. Basically, from the issues of economic, social, and moral self government to the issues of free and open political debate, these are eternal issues because they are issues to be dealt with by every society, in every age.

The strategy of this agenda is based on the reality that the hearts and minds of the people are always the driving force in any of the upward or downward spirals of government. Not only must hearts and minds be won over to effect change, but changes in the law can in turn affect hearts and minds, which can then bring further change. That spiral strategy based on the hearts and minds can be one going up, or one going down. Most of the experience of government, in this nation and the larger world, is one of downward spirals. We have a chance to start an upward spiral, where one good change can prepare and enable the next change of heart, which can prepare and enable the next. The positive results of this kind of government, in terms of peace, freedom, prosperity, and happiness are potentially far greater than with any other form of government.

Once we establish Local Community Moral Self Government, we will find that it is not a panacea for the problems of human government. Crime and corruption will continue, with various communities having varying degrees of success in preventing political corruption. While some instances of outright oppression will probably occur in a system of LCMSG; that is not the final word. In such a nation, activists throughout the country would arouse the people's attention in the direction of the oppression, so they would take the necessary actions to end it. It takes a lot of work to make a free system of government work; a lot of thought and action, on an ongoing basis, from a lot of dedicated citizens, for our system of free self government to work, but it is worth the effort when it does function properly. Getting a system of liberty initiated, and then keeping it moving, will most decidedly not be easy or short work, but it is a task that we might be able to accomplish, if we really want to do so.

Shortly after the U.S. Constitution was written, some of the authors had to admonish overly enthusiastic citizens who bragged that politically speaking, the Constitution was a "Machine that would go of itself." The founders involved were right to reject the idea that the Constitution, or any form of government, can ever be "machines that can go of themselves."

That sentiment of wanting a government on auto pilot is precisely where a democratic republic begins to be corrupt. The reality is that the establishment of justice rests solely on the shoulders of the people, and is completely dependent upon their efforts. Anything that diminishes that consciousness of having a personal duty to stand up for justice, or causes citizens to be willing to "let George do it" regarding the matters of politics, government or justice, is something that inevitably leads to bad government and injustice.

The internal debate we Americans have been going through the last seventy plus years is eerily similar to an internal debate the Ancient Israeli's had about government. At the time, Israel could be said to not even have a standing government. The land had been divided between the tribes and families generations before, and a system of Judges prevailed, where respected and learned men in a neighborhood were called on to judge civil matters between people, with the more difficult cases sent up to higher courts. In case of invasion or corrupt judges, the prophets were to sound the call, and the people would thereby be inspired to right the wrong and or defend the nation.

That Ancient Israeli system was up and functioning, even though it would undoubtedly have functioned much better if they had ever carried out the Divine mandate to give the original allotment of land back to the original families every generation. (Year of Jubilee.) Nevertheless, the Israeli people rejected this system, and told the Prophet Samuel to get them a King, Consider these words from I Samuel 8:4-7, 9, 19-20.

.

"Then all the elders of Israel gathered themselves together, and came to Samuel unto Ramah.

And said unto him. Behold, thou art old, and thy sons walk not in thy ways: now make us a king to judge us like all the nations.

But the thing displeased Samuel, when they said, Give us a king to judge us. And Samuel prayed unto the Lord.

And the Lord said unto Samuel, Hearken unto the voice of the people in all that they say unto thee: for they have not rejected thee, but they have rejected me, that I should not reign over them."...

"...Howbeit yet protest solemnly unto them, and shew them the manner of the king that shall reign over them...."

"Nevertheless the people refused to obey the voice of Samuel, and they said, nay, but we will have a king over us;

That we also may be like all the nations; and that our king may judge us, and go out before us, and fight our battles."

The similarities between ancient Israel and modern America is that in both cases the people started with a system of government that put the responsibility for justice directly on the people, and therefore required a lot of activity on the part of the masses for the system to work. The further similarity is that both peoples bought into the temptation to put the government on some sort of automatic pilot, to transfer the responsibilities of government from their shoulders over to some elite authority that would take care of things for them. In ancient Israel, they wanted a king. In America, since the time of FDR, we think that all problems are the province of the federal government, and the only duty we the people have is to vote correctly every other year. Even that minimal level of citizenship is scorned. Most people think the only relationship they have with government is as dependent consumers or grousing taxpayers.

Let's look at the truth that the establishment of justice is solely on the shoulders of the people from another angle. The constitution of the old Soviet Union was a marvelous statement of rights and freedoms. Unfortunately, the people were not in a position to insist that it be followed, so it became a hollow façade. The point is that any system of law, no matter how eloquent or well stated, is only as good as the spirit of justice in the hearts of the masses makes it. If that spirit is thriving, all is well. If it is dormant, then justice is probably much denied. If the masses realize that getting justice is based on their participation in government, then we can expect justice to be sure. Anything that reduces that realization that justice must be defended by "me", that plays into the human failing of thinking that we can put the dispensing of justice in a bottle and it will be automatic after that, or that any government can be "a machine that will go of itself" is something that leads inevitably to injustice and oppression.

We can see at this point how the desire of the masses to escape the responsibilities and burdens of self government dovetails perfectly with the elites and their "politics of self deification". Every time the people abandon some aspect of self government, every inch they flake off, we can be certain there is someone waiting in the wings, eager to fill the void and play the role of a god ruling over us. That is probably how all previous civilizations declined.

So even though centralized government seems like a viable shortcut to that land of milk and honey, centralized governmental and economic structures carry within them the much greater hazard of elitist control of society, with all the abuses that accompany it. It must be conceded that Local Community Moral Self Government can be risky, and has sometimes led to confrontation and suffering and that all human suffering is bad. Nevertheless, the amount of human suffering that has been caused by elitist, over-centralized governments so dwarfs the problems potential with LCMSG when the holocausts and modern total wars are considered, that it barely warrants comparison.

The point is that every kind of government has some built-in risks. It is wise to consider which system of government offers the least risk, and the most promise of a brighter future.

Every form of government involves a form of faith, whether that is faith in the people, faith in God, or faith in some distant elite. Given the track records of the various forms of government, the clearly wise choice is that of the locally controlled self governing republics in a federated national structure of checks and balances.

This manifesto, revealing as it does the intertwined nature of big government and big business in the fascist oligarchy that rules over us is not intended to raise a revolution. Rather, it offers an alternative to the decline into totalitarianism that seems to loom as our inevitable fate. It presents a unifying vision of how liberty did, can, and should work in this nation, and it offers an agenda that would give us a fighting chance to get there. When the inevitable crisis comes to a head, and it looks like we must choose between collapse and totalitarian despotism, this manifesto offers a third choice.

The major point is that the only way we can get a handle on the huge problems of over-centralized government, out of control corporations and a runaway industrial revolution, is by embracing the fact that we have to raise ourselves to a much higher level of moral consciousness. Furthermore, the only way to achieve that moral uplift is by a return to the Local Community Moral Self Government this nation was founded upon.

Make no mistake, this will not be an easy change to make, nor will the path of LCMSG be easier, at least in the short run, than staying on our present course. It has been said that America is the exceptional nation. This "American Exceptionalism" will be put to the acid test in this case. No nation in history has ever come to the brink of decline and turned back toward freedom. Always before, they had to endure complete collapse before they recognized what they had lost. If we do that, it will be too late. But it is, as stated, an open question whether or not we are mature and exceptional enough to go against the grain of history.

Let's look again at the definition of revolution presented earlier. Revolution: To consider the long sweep of history, whether local, state, national, or global; figure out what we did wrong and stop doing it; figure out what we did right, do more of it, and then carry on. To the discerning ear, this sounds like a process of societal repentance, which it is. What's more, repentance, which essentially means to turn away from, on both an individual and community level, is exactly what is being called for here. If we are to avoid despotism, oppression, and virtual slavery, we simply must turn away from the false paradise of libertine socialism we have been seduced into embracing.

While this change won't be easy, when we stop and consider our position, we are sitting here with a handful of aces, but we are too demoralized and intimidated to play our cards. We are similar to that smart rat, still stuck in the titanium cage, a gilded cage of libertine socialism so sure that we can't succeed, that we never even try. This is silly, because there is much reason for hope.

The first cause for hope is that the moral decline which has beset our nation has largely been driven from above, and doesn't reflect the true moral status of the people. Our decline has not been driven by the corrupt hearts of a corrupt people, but has instead been driven from above by self anointed elites. They have been twisting the Constitution out of all recognition, and then using dubious court rulings, and the intoxicating power of modern media to debauch us. Additionally, anyone who attempts to buck the trend, to raise moral children, and infuse traditional morality into their hearts, is threatened and harassed by that same elite government. We are better than that, and if we didn't consider ourselves bound by those dubious court rulings, we could run this nation in a much more righteous manner.

What's more, actually moving in the direction of LCMSG would enable us to find a much healthier political equilibrium, with a natural ruling coalition in power. Today, that ruling coalition is hopelessly divided between left and right. On the right, those who desire a moral, righteous nation are marginalized and obliged to form common cause with the forces of greed and militarism. On the left, those who want a fair, economically just, and peaceful society are obliged to form common cause with the forces of socialism and debauchery. If loosed from the present unhealthy political equilibrium, those two groups would find their way to each other, and discover that those who want a fair, just, peaceful, and morally righteous society are in the vast majority. At the same time, those who still desire a licentious, debauched society would be free to form together in communities. But as explained earlier, since they would then have to pay for all their own problems, they would probably find they had to modify their desires to survive as a community.

The other major cause of hope is the power of the media. While it has mostly been used to keep us in the dark, the most natural use it can be put to is to shine the light of truth on things.

If we used it that way, it would dispel a lot of darkness, very rapidly. What's more, like a group of people stuck in a pitch dark cave, even a small candle can make a huge difference. Even if that candle is lit for only a short moment, it can still be a great aid, revealing the basic layout of the situation before the darkness returns. So any way that we can use the media to shed light on the problem will help the people.

In addition, there are all those methods of little freedoms mentioned earlier, like less restrictive housing, and transportation, education, medical care, and so forth. An entire universe of solutions would be in our hands, not prohibited to us by a distant government, if we chose to move in the direction of Local Community Moral Self Government. So, while the task of establishing LCMSG, thereby solving our myriad problems seems daunting at first glance, it is actually quite achievable. We merely have to be bold enough to play the aces in our hand.

Let us take a long look at that old Model "T" our granddad left under the tarp in the back yard. Sure, it's rusty, and some fools have abused it and used it in ways it wasn't intended to be used, but with some oil, elbow grease, and loving care, it can be brought back to life, better than ever. Thankfully, our Constitution still stands, and can be revived and returned to its original use, if we really want to, and are willing to insist on it.

The ominous times we face are similar to the times faced by the writers of the Constitution, and offer similar challenges and promise. We, like the Americans of 1787, are still in a state of relative peace and stability. We, like they, can look at the long sweep of history, and make reasoned, un-panicked, decisions about how to proceed. We can consider which policies and forms of government are most likely to produce the peace, justice, liberty and prosperity we all desire. Like our predecessors, we can see that our future happiness is going to depend on our ability to put a solid government together today. In 1787, they could see why they were doing what they were doing, with a good idea of how it would work. As Malancton Smith said, June 20, 1788, "We were now in that stage of society, in which we could deliberate with freedom;- how long it might continue, God only knew." [16]

We are in the same position today.

As we start to work on that old model T, let's open up the hood, and take a close look at the engine. Let us now deeply consider one of the most important writings in history, the first section of the Declaration of Independence. As we do, there will be a few insertions to clarify how it relates to present day.

"When, in the course of human events, it becomes necessary for one people to dissolve the political bonds which have connected them with another, and to assume among the powers of the earth, the separate and equal station to which the laws of nature, and nature's God entitle them, a decent respect to the opinions of mankind requires that they should declare the causes which impel them to the separation."

To be clear, this is not calling for "dissolving the political bonds" with the present government, but rather that we have been on the wrong trajectory, or path, one of a declining spiral, for about 150 years, and that we have to get back on the right path.

"We hold these truths to be self-evident:- that all men are created equal; that they are endowed by their Creator with certain unalienable rights; that among these are life, liberty, and the pursuit of happiness. That to secure these rights, governments are instituted among men, deriving their just powers from the consent of the governed; that whenever any form of government becomes destructive of these ends it is the right of the people to alter or abolish it, and to institute a new government, laying its foundation on such principles, and organizing its powers in such form, as to them shall seem most likely to effect their safety and happiness."

It is obvious that this government has become destructive of those good ends. This manifesto offers a plan to alter it back into a form that will affect our safety and happiness.

"Prudence, indeed, will dictate that governments long established should not be changed for light and transient causes; and accordingly all experience hath shown that mankind are more disposed to suffer, while evils are sufferable, than to right themselves by abolishing the forms to which they are accustomed. But when a long train of abuses and usurpations, pursuing invariably the same object, evinces a design to reduce them under absolute despotism, it is their right, it is their duty, to throw off such government and to provide new guards for their future security."

Was this long train of abuses and usurpations the result of a “design” (another word for conspiracy)? Maybe, maybe not, and beside the point, since we have but to get back on the right path.

The “Declaration” talks of our “duty”. This is, of course, a duty we owe first of all to ourselves, each other, and our descendants, but it goes much further than that. Since our nation is so rich and powerful, our duty to control our government is a duty we owe to all our fellow human beings.

What’s more, since our off the leash government has lead to an off the leash commercial empire, and a totally out of control industrial revolution which has caused much human suffering while converting humanity into a virtual cancer on the face of the planet, our duty also extends to the plants and animals, nature, the planet as a whole, and even to the Creator of all nature. We have an absolute, urgent duty to get control of the industrial revolution.

After the first section, the Declaration of Independence in 1776 contained a list of particulars detailing the complaint against King George III. This manifesto has detailed the list for our time.

We can see that our system of liberty has been usurped from us by a series of dire political changes: corporate personhood, federal socialism, and federal control of morality, which, along with the related peripheral changes that came in their wake, have effectively taken from the American people almost all the powers and responsibilities of self government. What’s more, we can see that we might be able to reverse every one of these changes, and restore to ourselves the reality and blessings of liberty. Further, with the promise of modern technology, we might improve on what the founders did, and by establishing something like the Open Media build a national foundation that could last another two hundred years.

May our Creator grant us the requisite wisdom, courage, faith, mutual understanding and respect to answer this challenge, and may God continue to bless the United States of America.

Footnotes:

[1.] *Democracy in America*, Alexis de Tocqueville, 1835, (J.P. Mayer- Ed., Anchor Books, Garden City, NY 1969), p.184

[2.] *The New Media Monopoly*, Ben H. Bagdikian, (Beacon Press, 25 Beacon Street, Boston, MA, 02108, 2004)

[3.] *The Anti Federalist Papers*, Ralph Ketcham, (Penguin Putnam Inc, 375 Hudson St., NY, NY, 10014, 1986), p.275

[4.] Ibid, p.242

[5.] Ibid, p.271

[6.] Ibid, p.246

[7.] Ibid, p.298

[8.] Ibid, p.268

[9.] Ibid, p.275

[10.] Ibid, p.279

[11.] Ibid, p.229

[12.] Ibid, p.347

[13.] Ibid, p.258

[14.] Ibid, p.324

[15.] John F. Kennedy, recorded address on occasion of new transmitter, USIA Greenville, NC, February 8, 1963

[16.] "The Anti-Federalist Papers", P.342

Other Books from Sword of the Spirit Publishing

2008

All the Voices of the Wind by Donald James Parker
The Bulldog Compact by Donald James Parker
Reforming the Potter's Clay by Donald James Parker
All the Stillness of the Wind by Donald James Parker
All the Fury of the Wind by Donald James Parker
More Than Dust in the Wind by Donald James Parker
Angels of Interstate 29 by Donald James Parker

2009

Love Waits by Donald James Parker
Homeless Like Me by Donald James Parker

2010

Against the Twilight by Donald James Parker
Finding My Heavenly Father by Jeff Reuter
Never Without Hope by Michelle Sutton
Reaching the Next Generation of Kids for Christ by Robert C. Heath

2011

Silver Wind by Donald James Parker
He's So In Love With You by Robert C. Heath
Their Separate Ways by Michelle Sutton
Silver Wind Pow-wow by Donald James Parker
The 21st Century Delusion by Daniel Narvaez
Hush, Little Baby by Deborah M. Piccurelli

2012

Retroshock by David W. Murray
Destiny of Angels By Eric Myers
It's Not About Her by Michelle Sutton
The Legacy of Deer Run by Elaine Marie Cooper
Will the Real Christianity Please Stand Up by Donald James Parker
Decision to Love by Michelle Sutton